PENGUIN BOOKS

EVERYDAY ETHICS

Joshua Halberstam teaches philosophy at New York University. His books include *Acing College* and *Virtues and Values: An Introduction to Ethics*. He lives in New York City with his wife and two children.

Everyday Ethics

INSPIRED SOLUTIONS
TO REAL-LIFE DILEMMAS

Joshua Halberstam

PENGUIN BOOKS

PENGUIN BOOKS
Published by the Penguin Group
Penguin Books USA Inc., 375 Hudson Street, New York, New York 10014, U.S.A.
Penguin Books Ltd, 27 Wrights Lane, London W8 5TZ, England
Penguin Books Australia Ltd, Ringwood, Victoria, Australia
Penguin Books Canada Ltd, 10 Alcorn Avenue, Toronto, Ontario, Canada M4V 3B2
Penguin Books (N.Z.) Ltd, 182–190 Wairau Road, Auckland 10, New Zealand

Penguin Books Ltd, Registered Offices: Harmondsworth, Middlesex, England

First published in the United States of America by Viking Penguin,
a division of Penguin Books USA Inc., 1993
Published in Penguin Books 1994

10 9 8 7 6 5 4 3 2

THE LIBRARY OF CONGRESS HAS CATALOGUED THE HARDCOVER AS FOLLOWS:
Halberstam, Joshua.
Everyday ethics: inspired solutions to real-life dilemmas/by Joshua Halberstam.
p.   cm.
ISBN 0-670-84247-8 (hc.)
ISBN 0 14 01.6558 4 (pbk.)
1. Ethics.   2. Social ethics.   I. Title.
BJ11012.H2364   1993
170—dc20   92–37174

Printed in the United States of America
Set in Granjon
Designed by Ann Gold

For my mother and
to the memory of my father

Preface

Chemists don't need to justify their subject, and neither do computer programmers, market researchers, or horse racing handicappers. Those of us who teach and write about morality aren't so lucky. In any conversation about what we do, we must explain what counts as a legitimate moral argument, what doesn't, and who decides. The problem isn't that so-called moral experts differ with one another—so do economists, historians, and physicists. The problem lies in the subject: Moral philosophy can be slippery, difficult to circumscribe. That's why ethics is both very hard and very easy; it's so difficult to prove your contentions but so simple to assert, with some plausibility, almost anything.

So what do we professional moral philosophers offer to the nonpractitioner? Experience. We've taken the time to think about these issues longer and more carefully than most, and that mental exercise is extremely helpful in analyzing moral problems. We may not always get you on the right road, but we can often direct you away from the dead ends into which we ourselves have stumbled. So if you're ready for some serious moral reflection, this book provides a head start.

Most of the issues discussed here are subjects of continuing debate within the philosophical community. As someone who contributes to that professional discourse, I know how complicated these discussions can get. But *Everyday Ethics* is not written for professional philosophers. It's written for everyone else (although I'd like to think that even academics will find something of value here). You'll find no technical analysis, no esoteric bibliography, no intricate formal arguments. Nor will you find scholarly footnotes, not because the ideas suggested here don't have their origins in the works of other philosophers, but because almost all do. In many instances, I can't honestly say how much is original and how much is derivative. However, while *Everyday Ethics* is not a treatise on moral philosophy, it's no less serious in its aims. And while it takes effort to get your ethics right, ethics can also be fun, as I hope this book demonstrates.

Authors share a special perk with Academy Award winners—they get to make public thank-yous. Since the opportunity is offered, I accept.

My thanks, first, to my friends and colleagues who served as such wise critics of the ideas I continually bounced off them. My agent, Agnes Birnbaum, helped shepherd this project from its incipiency. The book benefited from having, at different stages, two wonderful editors at Viking: Roger Devine and Dawn Drzal. My thanks to them both for helping me sail the book between the rock of academic philosophy and the hard place of an innocuous how-to primer. My wife,

Yoco, as always, assisted in so many ways, on so many levels. Ariana and Amitai—sorry for the false promises. Here I am writing a book on ethics and for months I tell my patient children that the book will be finished next week. Well, it was bound to be true one of those times.

We learn values first, foremost, and—often—finally at home. This book is dedicated to my parents and their extraordinary moral decency and compassion. As I began this book, my father passed away. My fondest hope is that he would have been pleased with this endeavor.

Contents

Introduction

Talk about ethics is everywhere. From all sides, we're told that we're morally confused and need to reestablish our values. Fine, but how do we do that? It's not as if you can simply declare that you're in control of your values and be done with it. Understanding your own ethics is hard work. *Everyday Ethics* aims to help in this endeavor.

Because this book is unusual in its approach, it may help to be clear at the outset about what it does and does not set out to accomplish. First, this is not a book about social morality. It is a book about *personal* morality—the morality of everyday ethics. Social issues are those problems you see every day on the news and read about in magazines. Affirmative action, abortion, capital punishment, foreign policy, tax redistribution, and the right to view pornography are examples of public policy concerns. You hear these topics discussed in high school debates, during political campaigns, and at the dinner table. They're important to you as a citizen, but they have little to do with your personal life. You, alone, can't change the law, nor does the resolution of these issues reflect on you personally.

But what about the quality of your friendships? What do you owe to your lover whom you no longer love? Why are your conversations so dishonest? Are you responsible for your anger? For your guilt? How important—be honest—is money in your life? Do you have to tolerate intolerance? These concerns of personal morality are some of the topics of this book.

The key to your everyday ethics, and the underlying theme of this book, is your moral character. Morality is not primarily about duties, about following rules that say, Do this, Don't do that. It is primarily about moral sensitivity. The pivotal moral imperative is not *do* the right thing, but *be* the right thing. If you have a decent character, if you care about intelligence, honesty, and compassion, you'll do the right thing as a matter of course.

The subject of this book is, in a word, integrity. In two words, integrity and responsibility. My aim here is to help you to integrate the many strands of your personal value system—to make it whole—and to take responsibility for whether you succeed. It isn't easy to achieve integrity, but that's what distinguishes the decent person, the *mensch*, from the rest.

This focus on personal morality echoes a sea change that's been going on recently in professional moral philosophy. For the previous two hundred years, academic philosophers thought about morality in social terms. Thousands of volumes were written explicating such theories as utilitarianism (which defines morality as producing the greatest happiness for the greatest number) or Kantian ethics (with its emphasis on duty). Emotions and personal character were of secondary moral interest.

That's no longer the case. Over the past decade or so, academic philosophers have rediscovered the virtues. Professional journals now abound with articles about the ethics of love and hate, the family, friendship, dignity, and pride. It's a rediscovery, because this domain was the primary focus of still earlier moral philosophy—of Plato, Aristotle, the medieval philosophers, Spinoza, Hume, and religious thinkers both Eastern and Western. It's a welcome return.

We desperately need to talk and think more—more candidly and more intelligently—about our personal morality. Now perhaps as never before.

The twentieth century has been an especially brutal period. Hundreds of millions of people have killed hundreds of millions of other people. In the name of their glorified ideologies, they have visited unspeakable horrors upon isolated individuals and entire nations. The effect of all this evil on our personal lives is subtle but profound. Our moral sensitivities can't help being numbed.

Modern life has also eaten away at the social structures we've come to rely on. For better or for worse, family life isn't what it used to be. Our friends are now scattered across thousands of miles. Increasingly, parents no longer live with their children. Our communities are fragile, exhausted, often nonexistent. Technology, too, has thrown us into a moral spin. Without a moment's pause, the electronic media beam their values into our lives; they shout so loudly we can barely hear ourselves think. Advances in medical research have forced us to reconfigure what we mean by life, death, and what we do or don't have the right to control. It's all terribly confusing.

But underneath it all, the same fundamental human tendencies reign. Some people are greedy, some caring. Some aspire to create, others to destroy. The only way we can work out our moral approach to this dizzying world is by recognizing our own inner moral workings. The great divide, then, is not between the moral and the immoral—that's easy—but between those who still care about morality and those who don't.

We've become very cynical. We call teachers, social workers, community activists, and those who devote their lives to helping others "bleeding hearts." What, then, runs in our own hearts? We tell our young not to steal because crime doesn't pay instead of telling them not to steal because it's wrong. We think an individual's morality is a matter of personal preference the way taste in dessert is a personal preference. We have transformed the exhortation "Live and let live" into "Live and let die," as if the welfare of our friends, family, and neighbors weren't our personal business. More and more of us realize that we need to get back to fundamentals. We need to think again about our values. We need to ask the important questions.

You certainly won't agree with everything you read here. (If you do, I've done something wrong.) At the same time, I've assumed that we share basic moral principles, such as that it's wrong to steal or cause suffering just for the heck of it. This isn't the forum in which to defend these basic principles with the complicated theoretical underpinnings of philosophy. We have too much direct work to do to allow detours into abstruse theory. (But I will ask you to join me in some philosophical analysis I've strewn along the way. Sometimes it's difficult for me to imagine that not everyone gets the same enormous charge out of doing philosophy as I do. I'm convinced, though, that most of us would see how much fun philosophy can be if only we did it more often.)

Morality has had a bad press. When you talk about ethics, people immediately slouch in their chairs and sigh. Oh, great, they think, here comes another sermon about how terrible we are and how we have to improve. Relax. You won't find any preaching here. I trust your intelligence too much for that. You will find, however, some inspirational writing, and that's intentional. We can all use an occasional pep talk as long as it respects our diversity.

Philosophy has been defined as "thinking hard," and my aim is to provoke you to do some hard thinking about your life, your values and your everyday morality. I certainly hope that some of what you read gives you new insights into your moral life, but even if it just gets you thinking hard about it, I'll have accomplished my goal.

PART I

The Morality of Relationships

1

Friends and Foes

Champagne for my sham friends; real pain for my real friends.
                                        —Francis Bacon

The one thing your friends will never forgive you is your happiness.
                                        —Albert Camus

May God defend me from my friends; I can defend myself from my enemies.
                                        —Voltaire

You've *been friends with Beth for years, but now the relationship has gone sour—at least on your side. You suspect, though, that Beth is oblivious to any change in your feelings. Do you still have to treat her as a friend? For how much longer? Has the friendship ceased with your change of heart or does the end need to be marked by some external event such as a frank talk or, perhaps, just the passage of time?*

Friends. So dear, so much trouble. Your worst moral headaches involve the people closest to you. Must you spend your vacation with the Robinsons even though you feel exploited when you do? Should you tell Linda that her drinking is starting to cause problems in your friendship? The list of dilemmas goes on and on.

When it comes to other everyday moral decisions, you can usually get away with following your whims. One day your principles tell you to give money to the panhandler and the next day some other notion dictates that you don't. You make up these personal rules as you go along; nobody notices, nobody cares.

You can't get away with this caprice when it comes to your friends. They make demands of you just as you do of them. Mess up, and you'll hear about it instantly.

The problem is usually misunderstood expectations. Because friendships are so ill defined, we often don't know a reasonable expectation from an inappropriate one. As a result, the morality of friendship is murky as well.

To begin with, we aren't sure who is and isn't a true friend. Compare friendship between adults with friendship between kids. Children baptize their friendships. "We're best friends," they declare. They even rank their friends in order of first, second, and third best. Then, one day, one of the best friends announces, "I don't like you anymore. You're not my friend," and the friendship is officially over . . . until next week.

Friendship for children has its rituals, as does adult friendship in much of the world. In our society, however, adults have no such formal friendship rites. There is no official marriage and divorce for friends, so you have a constellation of people floating in and out of your life, shifting positions in their orbit. You have friends you see regularly and friends you see rarely, old friends forever in the background, old friends fading away, and new friends coming on strong.

How do you know who's your friend? How do you know when a friendship is over? Without a demarcation that says now you're friends, now you're not, this friendship is solid, that one is decaying, we guess at our friendships and lose our moral bearings in the process.

The best way to assess the role of friendship in our lives is to jump right into the thicket. Let's begin this reappraisal by looking at the friends we don't like.

Do You Like Your Friends?

It's time to let the dirty little secret out. *You have friends you don't like.* We all do.

Can someone be your friend even though you don't like him? Sure—friendships are not only about liking. Obviously, you aren't going to be the best of pals with someone you despise, and most friendships with people you don't like usually evaporate, but you can sustain a friendship for many reasons other than affection: respect, admiration, loyalty, shared interests, and shared history.

How can you tell which friends you don't like? It's not easy to be honest about this. I recommend that you apply the *Schadenfreude* test.

The Schadenfreude Test

The word *Schadenfreude* captures an essential feature of our psychic life, but, unfortunately, there is no equivalent word in English. *Schadenfreude* is that happy feeling you get when you hear about another's misfortunes. It's the opposite of envy. Envy is your private dejection at seeing another succeed; *Schadenfreude* is your private joy at seeing another fail.

It's embarrassing to think about how common *Schadenfreude* is. Newspaper and television writers realized a long time ago they could make their fortunes from the delight we take at watching other people disintegrate. The joy is especially intense when the collapse takes down the high and mighty. Millions relished the Fall of the Yuppies.

The nastiest part of *Schadenfreude* is that we even feel it toward our friends. How do you feel—not intellectually, but in your gut—when you hear that a friend has lost a major client? In the case of some friends, you feel downright lousy; in the case of others, you feel a perverse pleasure.

Gossip thrives on *Schadenfreude*. You're on the phone describing the marital troubles of a mutual friend. Both you and your phonemate are sympathetic and want to help, but both of you also love the crisis. Neither emotion is faked: The sympathy is real, and so is the secret satisfaction.

Before you run to ditch your friends toward whom you've felt *Schadenfreude*, consider that:

1. *Schadenfreude* is part of the human condition. It's unlikely that you'll like all of your friends at any given time. But if you don't like a friend, you have to ask yourself what sustains the relationship. Sometimes there's enough there to make it worth it; sometimes there isn't.

2. Liking is a sometime thing. You have friends you usually like and friends you rarely do, but with all your friends the affection runs in cycles, burning bright, then dimming, then brightening up again. You can like a friend in the

morning, dislike her in the afternoon, and like her again in the evening. And she's still your friend.
3. Not liking *any* of your friends suggests a serious gap in your life. It's time for some difficult self-reflection.

Are Your Friendships Mutual?

This question goes right to the heart of any friendship. So many friendships sink because of the failure to understand how mutuality works.

Friendship, as we all know, is a two-way street. This mutuality is one of the ways in which friendship differs from romantic love. An infatuation can go on for years, unnoticed and unrequited. He adores her; she doesn't know he exists. Longing is part of romance, not friendship: A one-sided friendship is no friendship at all.

Be careful, though, not to confuse mutuality with reciprocity. Reciprocity is tit for tat; mutuality is sharing.

Whose turn is it to call, yours or Alice's? If you know the answer, your friendship with Alice is cool, maybe even dead. With genuine friends, you don't keep score. "The Andersons have had us over for dinner four times now, and we've had them here only twice, once just for brunch. We owe them a dinner." This is *not* the way friends talk. Friends don't "owe."

The concept of debt belongs to the language of reciprocity, not mutuality. We do favors for acquaintances and strangers, not friends—we help our friends because we care about them. Your friend is an extension of yourself. Just as you don't have debts to yourself and can't do yourself favors, so, too, it's inappropriate to apply these terms to your friends.

How can you tell when that critical mutuality is missing? Here, as a guide, are three types of insidious pseudo-friendships that demonstrate that lack of mutuality. These are friendships in trouble:

1. *the center-of-the-universe friend* who distorts the mutuality of interest
2. *the deflating friend* who distorts the mutuality of enthusiasm
3. *the presumptuous friend* who distorts the mutuality of resources

The Center-of-the-Universe Friend

We'll call her Serena and she'll call you . . . regularly. You probably have at least one Serena in your life. Serena calls and dutifully asks you how you are. That part of the conversation takes about a fifth of a nanosecond, after which Serena moves on to the subject of her call: Serena. She passionately informs you of all the sordid details of the latest chapter in her life. And we're taking *details*.

The Serenas of the world tend to be problem-driven. They are always in the midst of some crisis and expect you to agree that their current catastrophe is the most significant event now occurring in the universe. You become increasingly bored and angry with Serena's soliloquies. But you're polite and say nothing.

What can you do? This isn't just a question of etiquette—what you do affects people's feelings. You do have to make it clear, however, that you're tired of listening without being heard, of giving and never getting. Without mutuality, friendship is only a pretense.

How will Serena react? Be prepared for the end of the friendship. Now that your function as human backboard has ended, your services are no longer needed. But don't worry too much about Serena—she'll ensnare another sympathetic person. It might as well *not* be you. You want to be a friend, not a therapist.

The Deflating Friend

You're excited. You've just had a brilliant idea, or something wonderful has happened. You meet your friend and before long the excitement vanishes. Your friend is a deflator.

Some people have a wonderful ability to inspire and invigorate. You walk away from them with renewed optimism, feeling good about yourself. Their exuberance is contagious. The deflator has these qualities in reverse.

The deflator sees his role in life as Eternal Critic. Like an obsessive karate fighter, he goes into his critic's stance as soon as you show up with some enthusiasm. You've arrived with a new idea and he's determined to suck out every morsel of ardor you bring to it.

The deflator rarely attacks head-on. Sometimes he'll nod his head absentmindedly and kill your fervor with neglect. The conversation might go something like this:

You: Steven, I got this terrific idea. It hit me while I was on the plane this morning. It could make a mint.

Steven: How was the flight?

You: Fine. Listen! I had to go to the john something awful, and here's the stewardess pushing the cart up the aisle.

You know how they serve food on planes—no one can move, right? Stupid. Here's a much better way of doing it.

Steven: What, you leave the food in the luggage compartment? By the way, which airline did you fly?

You: C'mon, listen to the idea. No, you don't leave the food in the compartment. You install a conveyor belt. No more clogged-up aisles.

Steven: Above the seats?

You: Yeah. The details of where to put the overhead track, you can work out later. Okay, so you take the prepared food . . .

Steven: I don't mean to interrupt, but did you remember to ask your brother about Margie?

You: Yes, I remembered. Let me just finish the idea. You put the food on these conveyor belts and send it to the seat of the passenger who ordered it.

Steve: Interesting. It's too complicated, though. Anyway, I think I read something about this somewhere. Incidentally, are you going to Patty's on Saturday?

In a general way, your deflating friends want you to succeed—they are your friends, after all. Indeed, deflators can be extremely helpful and sympathetic when you have a problem. What they refuse to do is share your zeal. You can never rely on them to explore your ideas with you and help bring them to the next step. Be careful. Deflators leach away your passion and destroy your spirit. They lack the essential ingredient of mutual exuberance so vital for friendship. The next time you have a bright idea, talk to someone else.

The Presumptuous Friend

You don't know how many times you've lent him your lawn mower, but who's counting? He's your friend and friends don't keep tabs. Right? Right. So why are you feeling so resentful?

You wouldn't feel resentful if it were just the mower. But it's also the baby-sitting, and the car, and the help with the attic, and the books he's borrowed before you had the chance to read them. Most of all, it's the presumptuousness.

This friend never has the slightest shyness about asking you for things. As he once pontificated, "It never hurts to ask; all they can do is say no." He always expects you to say yes. You want your friend to have the lawn mower if he needs it, but the generosity has to be mutual. This friend doesn't go out of his way to think about your needs. He doesn't nurture the friendship; he exploits it.

Tell him how you feel. If you don't, the resentment will eventually kill the friendship anyway.

Are You Friends at a Distance?

You have a friend you haven't seen for years. No doubt you'd both be delighted to see each other again, but life keeps getting in the way. If the truth be told, over the past two years you've talked a lot more with your dry cleaner than with this friend.

You say the bond is still there, but you can't recall Amanda's new baby's name. You include Scott among your close buddies, but you don't know if his father is still alive. Sharon and you have a great time together, but you still haven't visited her new house. You certainly *had* a friendship, but do you still? Are you friends in name only?

Friendships need continuing dialogue, from banter to heart-to-hearts. They need trips to the movies, cups of coffee, dinners in and dinners out. If that's not possible, then at least they need frequent telephone conversations.

Most of our adult friendships are in desperate need of a whole lot more spontaneous, purposeless fun. Never rely on momentum. Friendships wither from lack of attention.

Special Friends

Most friendships are in a state of flux. Some of yours are on the way out, some are in a holding pattern, and some are still in development. You'll have periods when your friendships are intense or relatively unimportant, when you have more or fewer friends. (Recent evidence suggests that whether we prefer a few intimate friends or many friends depends on personality traits that are inculcated during childhood. Parents need to teach the skills of friendship.) You have friends who make you think and friends who make you laugh, friends for emotional discussions and friends for just hanging out with. But a few friendships stand out from the rest.

Old Friends

Among your closest friendships are your oldest ones—those that reach back even to childhood. The two of you first became friends for reasons that make no difference now. Perhaps you were neighbors or classmates. In many cases, were you to meet your old friend now for the first time, you wouldn't hit it off. You have so little in common: different values, different tastes, different aspirations. You might downright dislike each other. So why are you friends? Because what you do have is equally important . . . a shared history. After all the fights, the neglect, and the jealousies, your friendship has survived. That's a powerful connection.

The years of friendship have provided you with important *tacit* information about each other; you can quickly read each other's gestures, body language, and moods. You know each other's strengths and weaknesses. One friend has excellent judgment when it comes to money but atrocious judgment when it comes to people. Another has enormous sensitivity about spiritual matters but is profoundly irresponsible. You've learned all this the hard way.

Remember that historical bond the next time you wonder how a newer friend of yours could have a lifelong friendship with the jerk to whom you've just been introduced. And remember it, too, when you introduce your old friends to your new ones.

Your new friends meet your old friend Derek for the first time and don't like him. You aren't surprised. However, having known Derek for as long as you have, you see beyond his "inessential" defects. "You really have to know Derek well to appreciate him," you tell them.

"Life is too short" is what they tell themselves in reply. "Why bother exploring Derek's buried treasures? Maybe you can disregard the fact that he's arrogant, impolite, and pushy—you've overlooked these characteristics for so long now. You can ignore his faults, but why should we?"

And they won't, though you probably will. Old friendships have an enormous capacity to withstand heavy pressure, and they're usually worth preserving. But recognize, too, that even old friendships aren't indestructible. The past, as they say, has a vote but not a veto.

Interesting Friends

We enrich our lives by having friends with various interests. There's hardly a better way to enlarge your own outlook than by having friends with different perspectives. The best way to learn about any subject, other than direct personal involvement, is to have a friend in the field.

One of my close friends is an artist and, without question, I've learned a hundred times more about art from my conversations with him than I have from all the art books I've read. Spending time in his studio and accompanying him on trips to galleries and other artists' studios have helped me to develop intuitions about art I would otherwise never have had. Along with learning to differentiate between schlock and real art, I've seen firsthand the intricate wheeling and dealing of the art world. Books would never have taught me all this—especially the inside gossip. From my friend in the diamond business, I've discovered the shady labyrinth of that mysterious industry. My friend the cardiologist describes to me the wonderful world of bypass operations, and my television news producer friend has taught me why I should be so suspicious of nightly news programs. And so on, as no doubt you've learned from your own crew of companions.

Friends tell you the inside story. As you recognize with your own work or interests, you have to work in a field to know what's substantial and what's trivial, what's enduring and what's merely popular, who's really good and who's all hype. You can't get that kind of information from reading magazine articles.

Try to maintain friendships with people with different interests. If only by osmosis, you can't help becoming more interesting yourself.

Cheerful Friends

Happy friends make for a happier life. An afternoon with a morose friend leaves you dispirited for a week, and years spent with morose friends can make you joyless for life. No matter how buoyant you are, you can't sustain optimism if you're surrounded by pessimists. You know this from your own experiences. On those dismal days when you're down on yourself, you make a lousy friend. You're stingy with your emotions and ungiving. On the buoyant days when you're up on yourself, you're a joy to all.

Try not to get trapped by the perpetually angry and cynical. For every one of your friends who carries the weight of the world on his shoulders, try to have at least two who are lighthearted. The attitudes of your friends are contagious. If you have productive friends, then you'll become more productive as well—you don't want to be the deadbeat in the bunch. Similarly, if your friends are cheerful, you don't want to be the group downer.

You amplify your pleasure by sharing it. So do yourself a good turn: Get yourself friends who know how to laugh.

Best Friends

Who are your best friends? The friends who care about what's best for you.

Old friends, productive friends, happy friends can make

for wonderful friendships, but they're not, in themselves, the best of friends. While those friendships are based on shared interests and pleasures, the best friendships are based on shared values. To understand why, you need to rethink the meaning of friendship.

One of the first things you realize when you start thinking about friendship is how seldom you do think about it. We don't talk much about this subject. You can see how under-valued friendship is when you compare the attention it gets with that received by romance. Songwriters rarely write songs about friendship; few authors write novels about it.

The most dispiriting aspect of this neglect is that we don't even talk about our friendships with our friends. Again, com-pare this disregard to our treatment of romance. Lovers con-stantly monitor their relationship, celebrate its strengths, complain about its weaknesses. When was the last time you talked about the state of your friendship with your best friend?

'Twasn't always so. The biblical story of David and Jon-athan, the Homeric tales, *The Three Musketeers*, stories of old from around the world, all made much of friendship. Phi-losophers and social commentators weighed in with their analyses. They made it clear that while romance is the fleeting material of ecstasy and despair, friendship is the steady diet that sustains the good life.

Aristotle did not consider anyone happy unless he enjoyed a thriving friendship; he devoted more than a fifth of his classic book the *Nichomachean Ethics* to the subject. Appar-ently, human beings haven't changed much. What he had to say about friendship still rings true more than two thousand years later. He divides friendship into three categories:

1. *Friendships based on mutual interest.* This category includes your friends in the reading group, members of your country club, your colleagues, car pool associates, fellow congregants. These friendships make up a large part of our lives.
2. *Friendships based on mutual pleasures.* In this category are your friends with whom you enjoy hanging out. With these pals you shop, fish, party, visit galleries, trade recipes, and gossip. When people think of their friends they usually think of friends in this category.

    Friendships based on interests and pleasures are solid friendships . . . for now. But these friendships, says Aristotle, have no long-term security. As your interests and pleasures change—and they will—so will these friends.
3. *Friendships based on mutual values.* These are your truest friendships.

Gary is working twelve hours a day, in a desperate climb up a slippery corporate ladder. You admire his fortitude and determination, but you also think he's jeopardizing his marriage and spending too little time with his children. It's been months since he's listened to the music he so dearly loves. Gary's become impossibly serious about being serious. You know him well and you don't think this is the way he wants to live his life.

Should you have a talk with him? Of course. Is it your business? It sure is. When you care for someone, lover or friend, that person's self-interest becomes your own interest. What matters to your friend matters to you. Who decides what's in your friend's best interest? Admittedly, it's not entirely up to you, but it's not entirely up to your friend, either.

At any given time, you have a general notion of what your ideal life would look like. Without too much prompting, you could make a list of what you need to make you happy. You're aware, however, that these ideals will change. You don't have the same dreams now that you did fifteen years ago, and you can bet that you'll have yet a different set of aspirations fifteen years from now. The fact is, we don't always behave in the way that's best for us, and neither do our friends always know what's best for them.

Gary may believe that becoming regional manager will improve his life substantially, and he may be right. He may also be wrong. As his friend, it's your duty to help him think it through. Make sure Gary is honest with himself about what he wants. Does he fully understand the trade-offs?

Suppose he's convinced you that he has given the matter careful attention and has sincerely adopted a new set of values. You don't like those values. You think this new direction is not in his self-interest. In that case, you're obligated to try to turn him around.

Your job is to persuade, not to impose. You appeal to him as a friend who cares, not as a parent or enforcer. Moreover, your own values should be broad enough to allow for differences of opinion. Not everyone has to live his life the same way. Nevertheless, if you think your friend's new values are self-destructive and seriously misguided, then not only do you have a right to tell him so, you have an *obligation* to tell him so. This is difficult because it flies in the face of the pervasive notion that we have no business telling other people how to live their lives. In this case, it *is* your business.

"You do your thing and I'll do mine" is the ethics of strangers, not friends. The fear of addressing our friends' values is the reason many of our friendships are so shallow. We worry more about being polite to our friends than about engaging them. We let them (as we let ourselves) get away with laziness in their professional lives, poor self-esteem, underachievement in their relationships with their spouses and lovers, too little joy. We let them off easy in just those areas of life that really matter. You need your friends to tell you when you've lost your spark and are drifting into inertia, and they need you to do the same for them. You don't need permission to be intimate. *That you care about what is essential in your friend's life is your license for intimacy.*

Watch out for a trap here. Too many people gleefully equate their concern with their friends' values with the authority to become a preacher. You're a friend, not a guilty conscience. Make sure you're as eager to congratulate your friend when he's flourishing as you are to confront him when he's sinking.

Friendships based on values celebrate mutuality of character, not mutuality of temperament. You and your friend can have incongruous styles and dissimilar personalities, but if you share the same values, your friendship is firm.

The sixteenth-century French essayist Montaigne wrote this about his dearest friendship: "In the friendship I speak of, our souls mingle and blend with each other so completely that they efface the seam that joined them, and cannot find it again. If you press me to tell you why I loved him, I feel that this cannot be expressed, except by answering: Because it was he, because it was I."

When a Friendship Is Over

How can you tell when a friendship is approaching the end? It's actually quite easy. If you're wondering whether to remain friends with someone, your friendship is in serious trouble. To be able to judge the worth of a friendship, you have to step outside it. But you can't remove yourself that easily from a thriving friendship, nor would you want to.

An analogy to the parent-child relationship is helpful here. No matter how bratty their kids may be, parents don't ask themselves why they love their children. You'd worry for the child of parents who coolly calculate how much love their child deserves. When a friendship is flourishing, you can be angry as all hell with your friend, but the anger remains within the bounds of the friendship. Most of the time, it's precisely because you are friends that you're so ticked off.

When you get nothing but grief from the relationship and wonder why you even bother, it's a clear sign that the bond between the two of you is badly frayed, if not entirely severed. Your frustration will soon turn into indifference and the friendship will fade into the past.

Enemies

Our lives are populated with good friends and casual friends, acquaintances we like, acquaintances we dislike, and a vast multitude of people about whom we're indifferent. Some of us at some point also have an enemy. If you have an enemy, you know that enmity can excite your passions as intensely as your most profound friendship.

A formidable enemy can be inspiring. For many, the desire to best a rival becomes the central motivation to succeed. Hatred, however, can also become an obsession that undermines your emotional balance and perverts your judgment. It can make you petty and downright unpleasant. Regardless of the outcome, to have an enemy is to be involved in a powerful relationship. And hatred is more easily sustained than love. How do you make that relationship work for you, instead of against you? By choosing your enemy intelligently. No one *falls* into hatred.

On a certain level, you must respect your enemy; he or she must be worthy of you. As you know, the better your opponent, the better you play the game. That's true of tennis, chess, poker, and personal rivalries. The more substantial your adversary, the more substantial your efforts to outdo him, and the sweeter the success when you do. Ask yourself whether the person you hate so bitterly merits so much of your emotional attention. The proper response to a lightweight is indifference, not hatred. Make your enemy work for you, not eat away at you.

Three Enemies of the Imagination

Lifelong mutual hatreds are rare. More common are the one-directional rivalries that endure in your mind. Here are three such animosities that we all contend with in our imaginations, time and again.

THE OBSESSIONAL FOIL   You've been fired. Unfairly, of course. He thinks you're unworthy? Well, you'll show the cretin.

You take revenge . . . in your daydreams. In your fantasy, you drive right past the skunk in your sparkling new Rolls-Royce, looking as dapper and prosperous as your imagination will allow. You show him who won in the end.

Your boyfriend spurned you for another woman? He thinks he got a better deal? Now let him see you. That's you in the restaurant looking positively glamorous, sitting very close to an equally glamorous gentleman. Your ex comes over to say hello. You pretend not even to recognize the guy. Let the creep eat his heart out.

These revenge scenarios would be delicious if only they came true. You know how unlikely that is. You also know —and this is the frustrating part—that while you're spending all these hours writhing with anger, your boss or old boyfriend isn't thinking at all about what he did to you. He did his dirty work and forgot about it ten minutes after it was over.

Anger often includes thoughts of revenge. You're allowed to be angry, and you're allowed to fantasize about revenge— up to a point. Beyond that point, anger turns to self-destructive despair. After a while, the face of the target blurs and all you're left with is the venom itself, which poisons only you. So go ahead and imagine skewering the bastard. As with grief, hatred has its proper day—and then you have to move on.

THE INTELLECTUAL FOIL A milder but more enduring rival is your intellectual foil She's the one with whom you have a continuing, sometimes lifelong argument. If you're the political liberal, she's the conservative. If you're the rationalist, she's the religious one. You read something in the newspaper that supports your position and envision saying to your opponent: "There, you see this! Now what do you have to say?" You have an experience that confirms your side of the argument and inside your head you proudly lord it over your intellectual nemesis. You're scoring points all the time.

You carry on this debate whether or not your adversary is present, and she may have no idea that she's the target of your argument. More often than not, this rival is idealized. That is, you want her to have these particular views so that you can victoriously demonstrate your own. This endless match takes place mainly in your mind, where you're both fighter and referee. Not surprisingly, you ignore any contrary information that comes your way, thereby depriving your adversary of a clear shot at your position. It's a cheap way to win arguments.

Do you really need a foil to prove your point of view to yourself? Maybe it's time for a new adversary. Maybe you won the argument already and you don't need an opponent at all.

THE PERSONAL FOIL Your intellectual foil lives in your head, but your personal foil lives in your heart. Who is this person? It's the individual against whom you measure your successes and failures. It's the one whose respect you always crave. When you're in the midst of a losing streak, this is the person you most want to avoid meeting; when things are going well, you welcome an encounter so that you can flaunt your good fortune.

The personal foil, like the intellectual foil, is someone from your past whom you have elevated into a permanent role in your life. He or she could be a sibling, a parent, a former boss, or a former friend with whom you were once competitive. You never stopped competing.

You're in a no-win situation. Your antagonist has nothing to prove; only you do. Spending your life proving yourself to this imaginary foe is exhausting. You're the one who sustains the rivalry. You're the one who can end it. So end it.

A Final Word on Hatred

Hatred is not in itself an immoral emotion. We're told to love our enemies, but also to hate sin. It's part of the moral package. If you love justice, you despise injustice. If you revere fairness, you revile prejudice. If you value intelligence, you're impatient with stupidity. If you admire people with moral decency, you loathe those of evil character. Moral passion is double-edged. But hatred is riskier than love.

The asymmetry between undeserved love and undeserved hatred is part of a deeper philosophical asymmetry. It's worse to punish the innocent than to let the guilty go free. It's worse to cause an individual pain than to deprive an individual of pleasure. And it's worse to hate for no good reason than to love for no good reason. Undue love is foolish, but there are many worse things than acting foolishly. Undue hatred, on the other hand, can cause profound harm to both the target of your hatred and yourself. Which is why if you hate, you should hate very carefully.

2

The Morality of Romance
(and a Bit about Sex)

If love is the answer, could you rephrase the question?
                                                    —Lily Tomlin

People who are sensible about love are incapable of it.
                                                    —Anon.

Romance

All of us are under enormous cultural pressure to be romantically engaged every moment of our adult lives, but there's no moral rule that says we must be. Romance isn't for everyone, and not everyone who pursues romance succeeds. But when you *are* "involved"—and especially when you're at the edges, coming in or going out of a romantic relationship—moral considerations are very much at issue.

Love affairs find people at their most vulnerable, and misunderstandings lead to the deepest hurt. Where there is human passion and suffering, morality matters. *We need a morality of love to accompany the poetry of love.* It's often difficult to know how to proceed in a romantic relationship: Your expectations, desires, and principles pull you in opposite directions. You want to be considerate of those who care about you, but you don't want to be a martyr. You need to be especially honest with your lover, but honesty can be particularly hurtful. Rules don't help much here; understanding does. The more you understand about the dynamics—and self-deceptions—of romance, the more you're able to make intelligent moral decisions.

Our lives are suffused with love-talk—it's the central theme of our novels, poems, films, songs, gossip, and therapy sessions—but we still can't get a handle on the emotion. The concept of love is as slippery as the real thing. Indeed, it's this very vagueness that leads to much of our moral confusion about love. So rather than define the term, which is nearly impossible anyway, we'll examine those features of a romantic relationship that have a direct impact on ethics. To help focus our moral investigation, we'll explore one particularly troubling aspect of romance—its demise. We'll look at the morality of breaking up.

Here's our itinerary. First we present a moral dilemma about leaving a mate. Then we look at the delusions of romance and how they can distort our moral judgment. Following that, we take an excursion into the metaphysics of romance and what is morally special about the romantic relationship. Brief side trips are included. We return with a solution to our moral dilemma.

My Mate Has Gone Crazy—
May I Please Stop Loving Her?

Two in the morning is late even for me, a notorious late-to-bedder, so it took a minute or so before I managed to rouse myself to answer the door. David didn't even bother to apologize. He just walked into the living room, slumped on the couch, stared at the floor, said nothing for a half minute or so, looked up and shook his head. "Enough is enough. I've had it. It's the end of the line. And I feel like a heel."

David had been distressed for months now, but tonight something must have snapped. "I loved Pam. I still love her— the Pam I married four years ago. The Pam I live with now? She's not the same person. We all know she's extremely neurotic, always was. Last year she tried to commit suicide, but we thought we were over that hurdle. She's been drinking a lot lately and now she's really gone off the deep end. Tonight she told me that the headlights of cars were signaling secret information to her. Apparently, I was part of a conspiracy to kill her, but she and her allies were wise to our plot. She's in the hospital now."

David is not usually given to forthright talk about his emotions, but tonight he was. "I don't think I love her anymore. I feel terrible about it, as if I'm deserting her emotionally just when she needs me most. I keep thinking that I have no right to stop loving her now. Suppose she had some accident and lost her leg, or went blind—that would be no reason to stop loving her, would it? If you really love someone, you're supposed to stick with that person, particularly when things go bad, aren't you?

"So tell me, is it all right to stop loving someone because she's gone crazy? I'm not talking about abandoning Pam while she's in the hospital—obviously I won't do that. But I know I'll leave

*her as soon as I can, and knowing that makes me feel free . . .
and miserable."*

David's dilemma is a *moral* dilemma. He's worried, admirably, about acting decent in this crisis. He also understands, correctly, that he exercises control over his love or lack of love: Not only does he want to *do* the right thing, he wants to *feel* the right thing. But David mixes up two separate questions—his moral obligation to continue to love Pam and his moral obligation to continue his marriage to her. As we shall see, these are very different issues.

He's an Angel/He's a Devil:
Maintaining Perspective

Love may sweep you off your feet, but you're still in control of where you land. No matter how you characterize your romantic love and romance, you're still responsible for the decisions you make.

Do you think romance is the be-all and end-all of life? That love justifies all? Or do you think romance is a delusion, no more than a massive media hype? Whether you revere romance or ridicule it, you can call on an army of social critics to come to your support.

In one corner are the love-bashers. This motley crew has little in common other than its cynicism about romance. Among the love-bashers you'll find radical feminists who regard romance as a male invention designed to keep women frivolous and emotionally busy with trivialities. You'll also find left-wing political theorists who view romance as part of the capitalist ideology that turns human relationships into commodities and keeps the rich elite in control. Joining these denigrators are some from the camps of the religious. Peel away the romance, they warn, and you find naked lust. Your devotion belongs to God, they preach, not other human beings.

In the other corner stand the love-adulators. These romance-boosters see love as "the poetry of the senses" and the highest of all human achievements. It's love, sweet love, that makes the world go 'round. Those who have loved and won know that love does conquer all, and damn the cynics who think otherwise.

The center of the ring between these two views of love is broad, and it's the rational place to stand. Love is a genuine emotion, not artifice as the skeptics would have us believe. But love is not a passion that must obliterate all other judgments, as the starry-eyed romantics suggest. We choose not only whom to love but how to love, and our willingness to distort objectivity is our choice as well . . . even when we're in love. Sometimes we permit this distortion at our own moral peril.

Both passionate affection and passionate repugnance warp reality. If love is blind, so is hatred. When you love someone, everything about that person is enchanting. "I love the way his nose crinkles when he smiles. He has this adorable bald spot and his giggle is just precious." Warts become positively endearing. Conversely, when you hate someone, everything about her grates on you. You can't stand the way she eats, the way she laughs, the way she walks, the way she talks. Yesterday's delightful birthmark is today's revolting deformity. You're charmed by your mate's every characteristic one day and totally repelled the next. Your mate didn't change; your feelings did.

The poets characterize love as a form of mental disease. To be in love is to be *crazy* about someone; you go "completely gaga" over your new paramour. (With some people, this sudden loss of objectivity is grounds for suspicion. You probably have at least one friend who manages to fall desperately in love once a month. "This one's for real," she insists, for the fifth time this year. Is she unusually romantic or does she use the word "love" with unusual ease?) By all means, allow your romantic passion the eccentricity it deserves, but don't overdo it. If you elevate your lover to a cut above perfection, you're setting yourself up for an unpleasant fall. Hatred, too, warps our judgment. Despite how you feel now, the way he holds a spoon doesn't make him as barbaric as Genghis Khan.

Love or Lust?

When we want to deflate our teenagers' infatuations, we tell them they're "in lust, not in love." That's a distinction we raise with our friends, too, when we disapprove of their latest affair, and even to ourselves when we honestly appraise our own romantic stirrings. Lust, we say, is one thing; love is something else entirely. But what's the distinction between love and lust? At root, are they really different?

Yes, they are, and here's one important difference: The object of lust is *fungible,* but the object of love is not. An object is fungible when you can replace it without any change in value. For example, the dollar bill in your pocket is fungible—you don't mind exchanging that particular bill for another of equal tender. The dollar is not fungible for you, however, if it was given to you by your grandfather on his deathbed and you promised to keep it forever. When you're in lust, you're attracted to a person's physical features, and anyone else with the same attributes would do as well. The object of your arousal is fungible—there are lots of people out there who can satisfy your sexual cravings. Love, on the other hand, allows no substitutions. *You aren't in love with Harry's qualities, you're in love with Harry.* You won't fall in love with just anyone who has his wonderful qualities. It isn't Harry's smile that you love, it's the smile on Harry; because you love Harry, you love that smile. Harry is not fungible.

What happens when the person you love undergoes a change? Suppose Harry gains thirty-five pounds? The lust may be lost, but the love remains. A heavier Harry may no longer turn you on sexually, but he's still the Harry you love. Shakespeare had this quality of endurance in mind when he wrote:

> . . . *Love is not love*
> *Which alters when it alteration finds,*
> *Or bends with the remover to remove:*
> *O, no! it is an ever-fixèd mark,*
> *That looks on tempests and is never shaken.*

Love, but not lust, is supposed to withstand a tempest, let alone a mere gain of thirty-five pounds. Whether it can withstand an *essential* change of personality is another matter, as we shall soon see. (As you can tell, we're on the way to solving David's dilemma.)

Another important difference between love and lust—this one more of degree than kind—is the extent to which we exercise control over these feelings. Why are we physically attracted to one person but not another? No one has yet figured out the biology of desire, but there's no question that we physically respond in very definite patterns without much mental deliberation. We use physical metaphors, too, when we talk about romance. "There was great chemistry between us," we say. Romance, however, is more an activity of the head than the genitals. We have a lot more control over our emotional affections than over our physical desires.

Falling in love is a decision, and a decision for which we are responsible. Decide that this is the year you find love, and there's a good chance that you will. Rule out love this year and love is effectively ruled out. People regularly make conscious decisons to close down their romantic urges at the conclusion of a wrenching affair or when a spouse dies. We determine whether to allow lust to turn into love.

Jackie is well aware of the tingle she feels every time she's near Ron. Knees do weaken, she notices with some surprise. Jackie also reminds herself that Ron is her best friend's husband and strictly out of bounds. Jackie won't let the feeling develop and suppresses the tingle and the knee-weakening. Were they single, she would certainly allow herself to fall in love with Ron, but not in this situation. Although she might not articulate it, Jackie is making a moral decision. Another woman with different moral views might decide differently.

We Are the World

Romantic relationships have two parts—the romance and the relationship. You choose whom to fall in love with and you choose whether to proceed with the relationship. When it works out—and, of course, it isn't only up to you—you and your lover create a new entity: the couple. The two of you move from a "you" and a "me" to a "we" and speak of an

IS ROMANCE UNIVERSAL?

Don't expect a definite answer from anthropologists or cultural historians—they've been fighting over the question for years. We do know that love stories have been around a long, long time; you'll find romance in much of the world's classic literature, including the Bible. Some scholars contend, however, that for most of human history, romance was the province solely of royalty and the nobility, for only the rich had the leisure to pursue such adventures; everyone else was too busy trying to survive. Moreover, what looks to us today like romance is often something else. For example, the capture of Helen of Troy precipitated a war not because her brokenhearted lover longed for her sweet caresses but because he wanted his property back.

The standard view holds that romance as we now know it originated with the knights errant and troubadours of the late Middle Ages. As the forlorn but brave knight marched off to battle, he would hide under his armor a memento of the woman he loved —usually a woman married to someone else. His beloved, for her part, wore a locked chastity belt. This was consuming love, not consummated love . . . and the basic narrative of Western romance.

This is the formula: Boy meets girl. Boy falls in love with girl, and girl with boy. The trouble is this is forbidden love—our hero and heroine belong to

> different spouses, feuding clans, hostile classes, or an-
> tagonistic religions. But love prevails. Disregarding
> the danger, our young lovers embrace one another.
> Then one or both die. End of story. Here you have
> the underlying plot of romantic tales from *Romeo and
> Juliet, Tristan and Isolde,* and the story of Abelard and
> Héloïse to *West Side Story, Love Story,* and ten thou-
> sand romance novels and movies.
>
> When anthropologists read these stories to people
> in non-Western cultures, they are met with utter
> amusement. "What's the big deal?" their listeners
> want to know. "If hooking up with Juliet is so much
> trouble, why doesn't Romeo just get a different girl?"

"us" against the world. Let's see how this entity develops.

Love expands self-interest to include another person. Parents are sincere when they tell their children, "If you're happy,
I'm happy," and true lovers feel the same way toward each
other. What delights and interests your lover delights and
interests you. What harms your lover harms you as well.
When you root for your mate, you also root for yourself. But
the self-interest of a romantic relationship encompasses even
more. It includes not only the other person, but also this new
"we." Each of you cares not only about the other but also
about the love, in itself, that you share.

The "we" takes nurturing, and being in love isn't enough
to maintain the relationship. Two people can love each other
without becoming a couple. They love each other from afar,

say, but neither knows about the other's affections, or if they do know of each other's feelings, they may not have the opportunity to plan jointly as a team. They love each other, but there's no "we" in their lives. Therefore, the fate of a romantic union isn't identical to the fate of each of the participants. It has a life and death of its own. The individual lovers can thrive while the unit decays, or the individual lovers can have hard times while the relationship grows stronger. With dreams come responsibilities, however, and lovers have obligations not only to each other but to their relationship as well.

The Solution to David's Dilemma

David and Pam no longer share a "we." As far as David is concerned, they have become separate individuals. David may still love Pam, but he no longer feels coupled with her. The relationship is over.

We noted that when we love, we love the person, not features of the person. If one of the partners gains thirty-five pounds or loses an eye, he or she is still the same person, and still part of this special relationship. Pam's case is different. It's not that there's been a change in her features, but Pam, the person, has been transformed. In David's estimation, her psychological disease has altered her personality fundamentally. He believes Pam is no longer capable of participating in that crucial "we." David still owes Pam his consideration. They have shared a special union and, as with friendships, a shared history has its special moral demands. A person can't just abandon this connection on a whim and without due soul-searching. But no one is shackled to the past, either. David may go his way.

FALLING IN LOVE IS ONE CHOICE,
PURSUING A RELATIONSHIP IS ANOTHER

Tevye in the musical *Fiddler on the Roof* asks his wife the big question: "Do you love me?" The question seems to come from nowhere. "Do I what?" she says in shrill surprise. "Do you love me?" he asks again, prodding her for a response. Finally, she answers that after twenty-five years of cooking his meals, cleaning his house, raising his children, fighting and laughing with him, she supposes she loves him. Her answer is tender in the context but philosophically off-base. Marriage, not love, is measured by the longevity of the relationship. And a reason to fall in love may not be a good reason to have a relationship.

We continually reproach people for falling in love for the "wrong" reasons. "How can you fall in love with someone like *that*?" we ask incredulously. The explicit charge is that the person is being hasty and confused, but our indictment also cloaks an implicit moral charge: This love shows a weakness in your character. Sometimes, when we disapprove of a romance we deny its existence altogether. Cindy tells us she's head over heels for the debonair South American she recently met. She mentions in passing that her new heartthrob happens to own one of the largest banks in Argentina. We also discover some unsettling information about the gentleman's history, both financial and romantical. "Cindy," we implore, "reconsider how you feel about this man. Love is blind indeed—you're blinded by all that cash. You think you're in love, but you aren't."

We need to sort out the tangled threads. One part of our judgment is correct: As her friends, it's our business to help Cindy choose wisely, for falling in love is a choice. The second part of the judgment is mistaken—just because we don't think Cindy should be in love with this man doesn't mean she isn't. We fall in love with people because they're beautiful, rich, famous, sexy, kind, or any other of a thousand reasons. The romantic inspiration might be frivolous, but that doesn't make the love frivolous.

I'm not sure what are "good" reasons to fall in love, but they're not always identical with the "good" reasons to begin a romantic relationship or a marriage. Too many, too often, confuse the two. We warn:

- Don't fall in love for beauty. Looks don't last.
- Don't fall in love for money. Money comes and goes.
- Don't fall in love for brains. You want a lover, not a conversational partner.
- Don't fall in love for social status. They won't accept you anyway.

This cautionary advice confuses love with other qualities of a relationship such as happiness, durability, and stability. Indeed, love itself might not be the best reason for two people to become a couple. Children through the ages have told their disapproving parents of their plans to marry. Their time-honored defense is: "But we love each other." And parents through the ages have answered, "Love is not enough. A successful marriage needs mutual affection, similar expectations, shared values. Love is only a small part of it." The parents may be right.

And a Bit about Sex

Sexual morality has a tortuous and varied history. Only a few rules seem to be universal—incest taboos, for example, are almost always enforced, and sexual intercourse is almost everywhere performed in private. After this handful of similarities the differences take over, and they are plentiful. Some societies, such as our own, prescribe strict monogamy, but 75 percent of recorded human societies are polygamous. Some cultures allow women a great deal of sexual license, while others still routinely perform clitoridectomies (to ensure that women are incapable of sexual pleasure). While young boys of Mangaia Island in Polynesia are formally instructed in the sexual arts by older women, many young boys in Western societies are taught that masturbation is evil. Sexual morality runs the gamut.

On the individual level, too, ideas about the dos and don'ts of sex span the range. And just as cultures have their own historical conditions which result in their particular moral rules, so, too, our views of sex are formed, in part, by our individual histories. Personal anxieties, frustrations, pleasures, and desires play a significant role in all our moral judgments, but especially in the formulation of our sexual moralities. It isn't easy to be objective.

I won't propose a theory of sexual morality here—I leave it to you to develop your own point of view. I do want to emphasize three questions about our contemporary sexual life that you should ask yourself as you formulate an ethics of sex.

1. *Does sex need a justification?* Most people, and this includes most U.S. Roman Catholics, no longer believe that sex must be limited to procreation. But most people, and this includes many who are cosmopolitan and educated, still believe that sex needs justification. You're allowed to eat spaghetti because you enjoy it, listen to Sinatra because you enjoy it, ride a bicycle because you enjoy it, but not have sex because you enjoy it. Sex for the sake of sex is not permissible. Sexual encounters, goes the argument, have consequences that make them different from these other pursuits. Pleasure, by itself, is not a sufficient justification for sex.

What *is* a good enough reason to have sex? For most, the answer is love. Sex must be *meaningful,* a term that implies an emotional connection accompanying the physical one. Sex, in this view, is a way of communicating these feelings of affection. So where traditional sexual moralities are tied to reproduction, modern sexual moralities are tied to romance. This isn't an argument for or against commitment-free sex. Again, that's for you to decide. But in formulating your sexual morality, be certain to ask yourself whether or not sex needs justification . . . and why.

2. *Do some people like sex more than others?* Of course they do, just as individuals have different tastes in other pursuits. What is less obvious is that these differences in individual temperament have ramifications for a morality of sex.

We're familiar with the conventional sexual morality that seeks to limit sex to specific practices, specific partners, specific settings. But sexual libertines sometimes preach their own brand of intolerance. For example, many who vociferously support the sexual prerogatives of homosexuals feel free to condemn "womanizers." And often, the same people who urge that everyone be allowed to have sex when and as often as they like mock those who don't want to have sex at all. Why the patronizing attitude? She loves rap; you love Schubert. He likes sardines; you hate the smell. You prefer lots of sex, he prefers lots of celibacy. If you want to tolerate other people's sexual inclinations, you need to tolerate them across the board.

3. *Is our current sexual morality satisfactory?* I submit that the state of our sexual life is a mess. Our culture has us in a perpetual moral muddle. Traditional morality expects sexual moderation, while popular morality urges a more casual, experimental sex life. For teenagers in our society these contradictory messages become an excruciating vise—damned if they do, damned if they don't. When it comes to sexual morality, most people proceed in varying stages of moral confusion.

As studies consistently confirm, a high proportion of

our population is unhappy with its sex life. People want more sex, better sex, more relaxed and enjoyable sex. (Why this widespread unresolved sexual longing? One alluring—but largely discredited—view is Freud's. He thought that without the sublimation of sexual energy into other creative pursuits we'd never get anything else accomplished: no sexual repression, no civilization.) Frustrated or not, we do manage to get along despite our sexual dissatisfactions. Life is full of inadequacies, and this is one more. The central question is does it have to be this way? As you formulate your sexual ethic—conservative or liberal—you need to address directly this less-than-happy state of affairs.

SEX WITH FRIENDS

What happens when you mix sex and romance with friendship? Trouble. As the discussion in this chapter shows, love and friendship involve two different sets of expectations. First, we should recognize that male-female friendships *without* sex are possible. Among the Nzema of southern Ghana, the Bangwa, and many other cultures, boys and girls form extremely intimate and cherished friendships that are never confused with romantic relationships. Friendships are highly valued and formalized in these societies, and friendships between men and women last a lifetime. Platonic male-female friendships are much rarer in our own culture.

In a recent study, only one of six married couples had a spouse with a friend of the opposite sex.

What about friendships *with* sex? Is such a combination viable? This question quickly dissolves into another: Which relationship is more important, the sexual or the friendly? We often answer with contradictory sentiments:

1. "I wouldn't mind sleeping with you, but I'm afraid it might ruin our friendship. I consider our friendship too important to jeopardize."
2. "No, we aren't lovers. We're *just* friends." (Or: "They're *more* than friends. They're lovers.")

Answer 1 implies that the friendship is more esteemed than the sexual relationship, while answer 2 implies the opposite. In truth, most of us would acknowledge from personal experience that the first answer is usually an evasion. The appeal to friendship is a convenient way to avoid an unwanted sexual encounter. It's also a commonly used tactic for terminating a romantic relationship. "Look," says the one ready to bolt, "I don't think it's a good idea for us to sleep together anymore. I love you—but not that way. I very much want us to remain friends, though." Romance, after all, is more valued than friendship in our society, and the commitment to it is taken more seriously.

It's difficult to honor friendship and romance simultaneously. Romantic relationships, we've seen, create a unique "we." Each partner belongs to this entity of "the couple," an exclusive arrangement that can be harmed by the entry of a third party. That's why infidelity is seen as such a threat. Friendship, on the other hand, doesn't create a unique couple. We belong to a group of friends, but rarely to a group of lovers—sharing a friend isn't like sharing a lover. You expect that your friend has friends other than you, just as you have other friends. (Notice, too, that romantic relationships can be one-sided. Love can be unrequited. Friendships, on the other hand, are always two-directional.)

When you combine sex and friendship you combine different obligations that often work at cross purposes. Sex with friends is, therefore, always risky. Is it impossible? No. First, for some people, sexual relationships need not be romantic ones. Second, spouses are often good friends to each other, sometimes best friends. The moral conclusion is that if you want to have sex with your friend . . . proceed with caution.

3

Creeps and Saints

A multicolored, chrome-plated hot rod is double-parked on the street. Mag wheels four feet high. Dragon painted on the trunk. With the muffler removed, the motor roars like a battery of cannon. Inside sits the triumphant driver. His neck, wrists, and fingers glint with studded jewelry, and his tattooed arms could pass for a wall at the Museum of Modern Art. He's very proud of himself. He sees me looking at him. At him and his car. He thinks I'm impressed and his grin grows wider.

Impressed? I'm thinking, What a creep!

The creep is a fixture in our lives. He dresses in various disguises—jeans, leotards, and three-piece suits—but you can't fail to recognize him. He won't let you. He's there blustering at the party, pontificating at the meeting, laughing ostentatiously in the restaurant, inevitably at the table next to yours. He's there, too, among the constellation of your friends. Alas, a bit of the creep resides in us all.

Creeps aren't evil per se. They can be law-abiding, solid

citizens, and generous to their friends. They can support all
the right causes and help the needy. But when it comes to
day-to-day interactions with other people, creeps come up
morally short. Creephood is not only a personality flaw but
a moral defect.

What makes someone a creep, a schmuck? What is the
creep's moral problem? Can you be a creep if you know you
are one? What are the telltale creep characteristics? We can't
adequately answer any of these questions without some theoretical investigation. We need a philosophy of creephood.

The Philosophy of Creephood

The key to the creep is his self-centered obliviousness.

Our assessments of our physical attributes and personality
traits depend on how others see us. We perceive ourselves as
attractive, entertaining, considerate, friendly, ugly, mean, bel-
ligerent, or boring if, and only if, other people see us that
way. Our dependence on the evaluations of others makes all
of us at least a little insecure.

If you're even minimally objective, you have a fairly good
idea of how others perceive you. You try to align your self-
image and behavior with your public image; you won't volunteer to emcee the next awards ceremony if you know that
people consider you a terrible speaker. To discover your public
image, you monitor the impression you make on other people.
We do this all the time, subtly and as a matter of course.

Not the creep. He's too self-centered to notice his audience, and when he does he misinterprets its response. He
reads his audience as he wants to read it. The creep thinks

he's another Robin Williams with a riotous sense of humor, while everyone else considers him a tedious jackass. He regards himself as the spiffiest dresser ever to have sauntered into a room, when, in truth, everyone else finds it alarming that a civilized adult could have such awful taste. The creep doesn't understand the difference between being clever and being obnoxious. He confuses charm with smarminess, confidence with arrogance, vivacity with plain loudness. The creep is too self-absorbed to bother with these distinctions. That's why creeps don't know they're creeps. If they were more self-aware they wouldn't be creeps in the first place.

This failure to read the audience also explains why creeps *tend* to be men. Women in our culture, and probably in all cultures, are far more aware of other people's judgments than men are; rare is the woman who's oblivious to other people. (Whether the reason for this is biological or cultural is an issue best not addressed here.) We have many nasty names for annoying women, but creep isn't one of them. Creephood, like stuttering, color-blindness, and baldness, is predominantly a male characteristic.

The Creep's Moral Problem
The creep isn't violent, but he is continually offensive. He may not lie outright, but he doesn't care much about the truth. He doesn't berate you directly, but he always manages to insult you. Creeps are stingy with their compassion and empathy. They won't make that small gesture that makes another person feel better about himself. They won't make that tiny sacrifice that saves another person a great deal.

The underlying moral defect of the creep is his lack of respect for other people. A pervasive inconsiderateness is the result.

This disrespect becomes clear when you look at the way creeps operate: how they talk, their opinions of themselves and everyone else.

The Traits of Creephood

Creep Spoken Here

Creeps are rarely the silent type. They're far too self-centered to deprive themselves of the music of their own voices. When they do talk, their creep mannerisms emerge unmistakably.

Creeps begin their sentences with "You see" and end their sentences with "Okay?" or "Do you follow?" You see, what the creep has to say is so profound that he must ascertain whether you, mere mortal listener, can comprehend his brilliant remarks—do you follow what I'm saying?

Creeps ask questions with the hope and expectation that you'll ask them the same question in return. The creep asks his victim, "Have you ever seen a bullfight?" "Have you ever been to Japan?" "Have you ever made it in a Jacuzzi at midnight with three women?" You answer, "No, have you?" Funny you should ask. The creep gleefully reports on his bullfight/Japanese/Jacuzzi experience. Your job is simple: Sit back and be impressed. This is a hard one to avoid. You sense that it would be rude not to play along by returning the question. You also figure that the creep will recount his adventures whether he is asked to or not. You're probably right.

"You think *you've* got problems? Listen to this." The moral insensitivity of the creep is most obvious when you talk to him about your concerns. You tell him about this terrific pain in your back and how you haven't slept in nights. The doctor can't figure out how to treat it. You could do with some sympathy. The creep listens to you for about ten seconds. "Yeah, I understand," he begins promisingly, but your turn is over. For the next twenty minutes he's off and running about how awful his back was last year and how he dealt with it. For him, your backache has long since faded away.

The creep can't, or won't, remain focused on anyone other than himself. It's not only your problems he refuses to discuss. He does the same with the positive stuff. You enthusiastically tell him the good news about the project you've been working on and how much it means to you. It means nothing to the creep. He quickly turns the conversation into a lecture on what you've done wrong. He tells you how he, the master, would have dealt with the situation.

Creeps turn all talk into arguments. The creep is convinced that this is the only way to make a conversation interesting. Mention that it's raining and the creep insists it's snowing. Agree that it's snowing and the creep will claim it's sunny. In his view, the whole point of human dialogue is the opportunity it affords to demonstrate his prowess at debate. The creep doesn't realize how boring these arguments are, and he also doesn't realize how deadly boring he is as a result. Unfortunately, many a creep has the rhetorical skills to draw you into his shadow-boxing performance; you waste a lot of time before realizing that, like it or not, you've been taken along for a ride on his ego trip.

Creeps are invariably pompous. Anyone who arrived in the United States at the age of three and still speaks with a British accent is a certified creep. The creep uses sesquipedalian words when simple ones would do—and he usually doesn't even know how to pronounce them. You, having the social grace not to correct him, let it pass.

Creeps adorn their sentences with particularly insufferable verbiage. The creep delights in long pauses, the better to impress you with his deep thought. He begins his sentences with rhetorical caveats: "Well, it seems to me," or "Your point's well taken, but . . ." or "I would be inclined to say." Inclined to say? He just said it. You ask him for the time and he answers, "Well, in actuality—it's an intriguing question—I'd venture to say it's about five o'clock."

Creeps are relentless name-droppers. This famous guy is his friend and that famous woman was in his class, and this star is a business associate. The creep with intellectual pretensions will allude to names in art, history, culture—anything to show his erudition. Half the time the reference is irrelevant and the other half he gets it wrong. A correlative creep habit is experience-dropping. We know this creep from the singles scene. He's at the bar, hitting on some woman. "I'm involved in the film industry," he tells her. Hearing this, you feel a sudden surge of nausea. (The sum of the guy's involvement in the film industry is probably that he saw *Death Wish* twice.)

Creeps talk to people as if they weren't there. This is an especially obnoxious creep habit. The creep uses you to talk to another person. Three of you are together: the creep, you, and his wife. He turns to you and says, "You know what her problem is? She never reads a newspaper. And then she wonders why she doesn't know what's going on in the world." Hey, the woman is right there in front of you. Why not try addressing her directly instead of talking about her in the third person? You feel extremely uncomfortable, but the creep couldn't care less. Creeps treat people as objects.

Creeps offer a running commentary on everything. You're discussing Claudine's new kitchen. You're in the middle of recounting her conversation with the contractor. The creep pipes up: "I think that whole contracting business is a fraud." Thank you. May I continue? But that's the way it will go all afternoon. No one is canvassing for his opinions, but you'll get the creep's judgments whether you want them or not. The creep personalizes every issue. He feels obliged to offer his endless opinions on the universe as you suffer in polite silence.

Creep Attitudes

Creeps own the best. If the creep owns it, it must be the best. His stereo is the finest available. His car is the best for the money. He doesn't own a car? Then owning a car is a stupid nuisance. His computer, his cigar, his running shoes, his guitar—there's none better to be had. Yours? Inferior merchandise, of course.

Creeps do the best. The creep flies planes. Conclusion: Flying planes is the most exhilarating sport in the world. He scuba dives? Then, of course, scuba diving is the supreme activity. His children are raised in the most intelligent way and his route to Washington is the quickest. After all, the creep always does it best.

Creeps know the best. Creeps have the most refined taste in women, wine, and song. If you don't believe it, just ask them. If the creep likes modern art, then only the philistine doesn't; if he doesn't like modern art, then only the fools do.

He declares which restaurants are wonderful and which poisonous, which books are classics and which are for illiterates, which film is the greatest of all time and which is a disaster. He decides for us all whether opera is an inferior art form. He tells us, too, what the President is *really* thinking. The syllogism is always the same: (a) whatever the creep fancies is superior; (b) the creep fancies X; therefore (c) X is superior.

Creeps think they're hilarious. Creeps are convinced that they have a sensational sense of humor. Unfortunately for all of us, they insist on showing it off. The creep delights in humor that dumps on the less fortunate. He is crude, rarely clever. He will tell an ethnic joke, sexist joke, or "cripple" joke without concern for the sensitivities of his listeners. For the creep, all the world's a stage, and he's the only performer who counts. It isn't just the inferiority of his jokes that's so annoying. The delivery, too, can drive you up the Sears Tower. A creep doesn't tell a joke; he shouts it—the only sound that's louder is his own laughter at the punch line. Somehow his mirth always seems forced, as if he feels obliged to demonstrate the proper reaction to his wit.

Creeps are cool. Remember "cool" from your high school days? The term captures the adolescent, egocentric creep mentality. Creephood flowers in the teenage years. You remember him back then, emulating the current screen tough or Mr. Suave. He'd dress the part, talk the part, live the part. Lacking the creativity to invent a role, the creep just borrowed his models from the media. It's amazing that he ever scored with the girls, though admittedly he sometimes did. Those occasional successes served to reinforce his role-playing and made him even more obnoxious.

Most of us gave up these swaggering poses soon after puberty, but the creep never grew up. He just swaggers differently now. His swashbuckling isn't Marlon Brando or James Bond anymore—though some creeps haven't even abandoned that yet—but he still sees himself as God's Gift to Humanity.

When the Saints Come Marchin' In

*Saints should always be judged guilty until they are proved
innocent.*   —George Orwell

The problem with the creep, as we've seen, is his persistent disregard for the feelings and beliefs of other people. The problem with the saint is just the opposite. Everything other people feel and believe is the saint's business. Creeps are tiresome and so are saints. Spending the evening with either one isn't anyone's idea of a rip-roaring good time.

So saints aren't a blast—what's the big surprise? The big surprise is that your reluctance to socialize with a saint poses a significant problem for moral philosophy. Saints, by definition, are morally superior people. It should follow that they're the best people. Are they? If sainthood is so wonderful, how come you don't want to be one? You don't want your friends to be saints, either, and you'd probably rather have your child grow up to be a film director or tennis pro than a saint. As candidates for an ideal life, saints don't get too many votes. It seems morality isn't everything.

AN EXCURSION INTO THE
PHILOSOPHICAL IMPORT OF CREEPHOOD

Creeps fall into an important category of the ethical domain: the obnoxious but not truly evil. These characters are far more prevalent than moral monsters, so we need to know where to fit them into the philosophical scheme of things.

Moral philosophy has traditionally divided human action into three categories: (a) the obligatory, (b) the forbidden, and (c) the permissible. It's the third category, the morally permissible, that poses problems. Most of your day is not spent fulfilling moral obligations or violating moral injunctions; most of what you do is morally neutral. You can wear a blue shirt or a green shirt, eat a pizza or a pound of brussels sprouts, sing an aria from *Madama Butterfly* or recite "Casey at the Bat." You have no moral obligation to do or not do any of these activities, and you won't be praised or blamed either way. These pursuits are not moral or immoral, but amoral.

How, then, do we categorize the guy who jumps into the freezing river to save the drowning child? You have no obligation to sacrifice your life for the life of another, and no one can blame you if you don't. But jumping into a freezing river to save a drowning child isn't morally neutral the way choosing to wear a blue shirt is morally neutral. You won't get a moral commendation for wearing the blue shirt, but you will for your sacrifice.

So we need a new category: behavior that is optional but praiseworthy. Philosophers have staked out this terrain and given it a name: the *supererogatory*. You act in supererogatory fashion when you act beyond the call of duty. Favors are supererogatory because you don't have to do them (otherwise they wouldn't be favors). Putting in that extra effort by working unpaid overtime is supererogatory. Volunteering for good causes is supererogatory.

If supererogatory acts are laudatory, why aren't they obligatory? Aren't we supposed to do the best we can? This is a problem for moral philosophers, and they have a lot to say about the subject.

Our present concern is those creeps. We have the supererogatory, a category of actions that are not required but are nonetheless praiseworthy. What we need is that category's mirror image—a class of actions that are not morally forbidden but are nonetheless *blameworthy*. It's not that you're prohibited from behaving in these ways, but you'll be considered a moral toad if you do. We can call these actions (the term is hereby coined) *suberogatory*.

We confront suberogatory behavior regularly. Rudeness is a good example. I'm not sure what moral rule rudeness violates, but it does demonstrate poor moral character and is certainly blameworthy. Obnoxiousness of all kinds is suberogatory. Heroes and saints habitually perform the supererogatory; creeps indulge in the suberogatory.

What's Wrong with Saints?

Why do saints make us so uncomfortable? A closer look at sainthood reveals some important lessons about the limits of moralizing.

Sainthood is a full-time job. A saint can't let his hair down and relax—there's all this suffering to attend to. He can't waste hours playing a game of Tetris on his computer, or spend the afternoon watching the Celtic–Laker game, or fritter away the evening reading mindless articles on fashion. Saints can't even spend time doing what the rest of us mere mortals consider useful activities, such as playing the tuba or reading nineteenth-century novels. Saints always have to be out there fighting the good fight.

Saints certainly deserve our respect. They have exceptional moral talent and dedication, and those qualities always deserve respect whether the skill is music, sports, or morality. Unfortunately, in developing his moral qualities, the saint often neglects other aspects of life. Alas, it's just those aspects that make for hearty friendships and romance.

We can divide saints into two categories: Saints of Love and Saints of Duty.

The Saint of Love is a natural. When she sees human suffering she suffers herself. Compassion is part of her constitution. She has no difficulty choosing a life of good works—she couldn't do anything else.

The Saint of Duty could easily have been one of the gang instead of a saint. Although she spends her afternoons catering to the sick and needy, she'd rather go to the movies or hang out with her friends. So why does she devote herself to saintly activities? Because she sees it as her obligation. The Saint of

Duty does what she believes she has to do, not what she wants to do.

The Saint of Love and the Saint of Duty act the same, but their motives are different. Neither saint laughs at off-color jokes (at least not in public), but the Saint of Love doesn't laugh because she doesn't find jokes about sex funny, while the Saint of Duty refrains because laughing at sexual humor is unbefitting. Neither saint will join you in a juicy round of gossip, or say anything sarcastic about anyone, or enjoy a Marx Brothers skit. Each has her own reasons: The Saint of Love won't engage in these activities because she gets no pleasure from them, while the Saint of Duty refuses because she believes they are improper.

Of the two saints, the one we most need to worry about is the Saint of Duty. Saints of Love can be a pain and a drag, but at least they mean well. Saints of Duty don't always mean well—sometimes they're just mean.

Remember the class tattletale? The teacher wanted to know which kid wrote on the board, "Miss O'Brien has a hot crush on Mr. Johnson." You all had the good sense to keep silent, all except ratty Lillian in the front row. Dependable Lillian. Always such a good girl, always ready to do just as she was told. Honesty is the rule, now isn't it? Somehow other moral sensitivities, such as not snitching on friends, never counted for much with Lillian. She was always clear on what her duties were, and the consequences be damned. I'll bet Lillian grew up to be a Saint of Duty.

Saints, and particularly Saints of Duty, are moral busybodies. They see every issue as a moral issue, and every moral issue as their personal business. Like a bottomless box of

Kleenex, they dispense judgment after judgment, endlessly.

Look at the way you dress! Couldn't you display a bit more modesty? You drink too much, swear too much. Why do you allow your children to read such trash? And while we're on the subject, the videos you watch aren't much of an example of decent taste, either. You could do with a better sort of friends—the ones you have are lowlifes. How can you spend so much time in mindless gossip with them? Aren't you ashamed of yourself?

Most saints are too clever to harangue you about all your faults at once. Sometimes they go right for the jugular; sometimes they deliver their sermons obliquely, coming at you from a tangent. Either way, their mission is to save the world, and that, unfortunately, includes you. It's hardly surprising that no one wants to spend an evening with these people.

Your Saintly Habits

Just as a bit of creephood creeps into each of us, so, too, a bit of the saintly lurks in us all. We each have our bêtes noires, our pet moral concerns. We're on the lookout for anyone who trespasses upon our favored moral terrain.

Take smoking, for example. Smoking cigarettes is truly dangerous, as any rational person recognizes. You should, of course, encourage your loved ones to desist, and young people, too. It doesn't follow, though, that you have to get on the case of everyone who smokes. You can safely assume that all noncomatose adults are aware by now of the perils of smoking.

They are or are not dealing with the habit as they see fit. It's not your moral domain. An unhealthy habit doesn't turn a person into a moral villain. As you'd expect, converts are the most offensive preachers. Ex-smokers need to resort to principles to withstand the temptations of tobacco. They often become Saints of Duty.

All crusades are holy crusades. Before you embark on a moral campaign, make sure you understand your motives. Make sure, too, that the issue is grave enough to warrant surrendering your sense of humor. Save your moral venom for major transgressions. Leave it to the saints to worry about the rest. We mere mortals have enough work to do just striving for plain old human decency.

PART II

The Morality of Expression and Emotion

4

Talk

*The trouble with her is that she lacks the power of
conversation but not the power of speech.*
                              —George Bernard Shaw

*If other people are going to talk, conversation becomes
impossible.*   —James McNeill Whistler

Language was given to man to conceal his thoughts.
                              —Talleyrand

We are talkers. When we aren't talking to people in the
flesh, we're carrying on conversations with them in our
heads—hectoring them, entertaining them, reprimanding
them. When we aren't talking to other people, real or imagined, we're talking to ourselves. We give ourselves little
speeches, mini-lectures, and provide an internal running commentary on our life. One way or another, we're always talking.

We converse, but our conversations are a mess of hidden
agendas, rationalizations, bullying, one-upmanship, covert

and overt prejudices, posturing, dodges, deflections, and deceptions. Much of our talk is boring, a waste of time. Are too many of *your* conversations aimless reruns? How often do you hang up the phone after a two-hour exchange with your friend wondering if anything was resolved? How often do you give yourself the same sermon, knowing it's utterly futile?

The root cause of pointless conversation is a systematic intellectual dishonesty. You should value how you talk, because how you talk reveals your values. We say we *value* honesty in conversation, but we hear less and less of it. The persistent dishonesty of the media has certainly debased the integrity of our talk, but our own moral laziness is also to blame. To talk well—and I'm not referring to public speaking or salesmanship skills, but to ordinary conversation—you need to engage in some honest self-appraisal. What's the point of this discussion? What do I expect to get out of it? What am I really trying to say? The payoff for this candid assessment is immediate and practical: Your conversations will be more productive and you'll avoid those pointless exercises in intellectual masturbation.

Our talk spans everything from pleasant chats to knock-down quarrels to soul-searching exchanges. To get a handle on this rich variety of talk, I've divided our discussion into conversations and arguments.

Conversation: The Three Levels of Talk

According to Fritz Perls of Esalen fame, conversations occur on three levels: chicken-talk, bull-talk, and elephant-talk.

Perls was interested in the psychological ramifications of these distinctions, but each has a moral dimension as well.

Chicken-talk is small talk, light and easy. "How're you doing?" "Seen any good movies lately?" "Been working hard?"

Bull-talk ups the ante. At this level, we exchange genuine information and our questions are personal. "Is your work satisfying?" "Are you happy?"

Elephant-talk takes us to the deepest realm of conversation. The content is weighty, and the questions are accompanied by the body language of dramatic gestures. "What do you *mean* by happiness?"

These divisions aren't hard and fast. The borderlines between the levels are blurry, and one person's bull-talk can be another's chicken-talk. Most of our extended conversations contain a mixture of all three, and we slide easily from one level to another. Nevertheless, you can usually tell what stage you're in.

At which level of talk are you most comfortable? If you're shy, chances are you prefer bull-talk and elephant-talk with intimates. If you're extroverted, you may excel at friendly chicken-talk with strangers. If you're like most people, you're probably better at one kind of talk than another, but you should strive for facility at each level. You bring a different aspect of yourself to each type of exchange, and each level challenges your moral integrity in different ways.

Chicken-talk is more important than is often supposed. It's the grease of the social wheel. The underlying purpose of chicken-talk is not to exchange information but to cement civility and community. *What* you say doesn't matter; *that* you say it does. Not knowing the appropriate chicken-talk

makes you uneasy, as you know from visits to foreign countries or interactions with people from different social strata.
Is it all right to say "Pass the butter, please" when everyone
is silent at the table? Is it improper to ask people what they
do for a living? Courses offered to people preparing to do
business abroad concentrate on chicken-talk. A mistake at
this level marks you as an outsider; your knowledge of
chicken-talk, on the other hand, signals that you recognize
the basic social cues of the community and that you're safe
to deal with.

Some people refuse to talk chicken-talk. They insist that
their time is too valuable to waste on "mere" small talk. They
act as if life were one long condolence call. You can't relax
with these people; their unrelenting intensity is oppressive.
They remind you of someone who never eats snacks, insisting
on a full meal or nothing at all, or who only kisses if intercourse is sure to follow. Most of us, correctly, don't wish to
go the limit at every encounter. People who think they're
"above" talking chicken-talk think they're above other people.
Invariably, they also lack a sense of humor. Their arrogance
masks a misunderstanding of the *point* of small talk.

Someone once defined a bore as a person who, when asked
how he is, tells you. "How are you?" isn't a question but a
greeting that calls for a greeting in return. You could just as
easily respond by saying "Good morning" or by raising your
hand or your eyebrow. Are you hypocritical if you say "Nice
meeting you" when you don't feel that way? Of course not.
This phrase is just another way of saying good-bye, not an
evaluation of the encounter. Only the grimmest pedant would
worry about its literal truth.

Chicken-talk is less about content than about the exchange

itself. Accordingly, we lie in our chicken-talk not so much with words as with our body language, our phony intensity, our misleading intonations. What grates on us is the extra enthusiasm, the insincere and unnecessary "I look forward to seeing you very soon." Relax with chicken-talk; this is talk you do with a smile.

Unfortunately, too many people can relax *only* when chicken-talking. We call these people shallow, and they are. People who can't talk chicken-talk have a problem, but so do people who can only talk chicken-talk.

Once we move past the pleasantries of elevator exchanges, we get down to bull-talk and elephant-talk. Here we invest more of our character, and the moral elements of talk come into sharper focus. Bull-talk and elephant-talk figure largely in both our conversations and our arguments, and the remainder of this chapter explores the integrity of our talk at these more intense levels.

Who Says Words Can't Break Your Bones?

"Sticks and stones can break my bones but words can never harm me." We constantly mislead our children with lies, but this little ditty belongs at the top of the list. Words can do a lot worse than break bones. They can break hearts, breed hatred, provoke murder, and command armies. Words can also console, inspire, and lift the spirit.

We have a *moral* obligation to take language seriously. Words have meaning, and when you bandy them about irresponsibly, they lose that meaning. The most horrible dictatorships have begun with the debasement of language.

Not everyone to the right of your politics is a fascist. If Pat Buchanan is a Nazi, that makes Hitler not as bad as

Hitler really was. Not everyone to the left of you is a Stalinist. If every liberal senator is the political spokesperson for communist dictatorships, then communist dictatorships aren't as cruel as some have been. The ease with which people use the terms "genocide," "holocaust," and "concentration camp" to refer to any and every questionable policy is scandalous. (Journalists are among the worst perpetrators of this verbal irresponsibility.) The failure to make distinctions perpetuates a dangerous lack of moral proportion.

Some people revel in name-calling because they think it adds drama to their conversations. But the law of diminishing returns operates here: Use shocking language often enough and it soon loses its shock value. Talkers who try to provoke by using outlandish language soon lose their credibility. Your word is your bond . . . treat it that way.

Listen Up

> *If silence be good for the wise, how much the better for fools.*
> —Talmud

The next time you're at a dinner party, in a meeting, or just hanging out with acquaintances, monitor the conversational flow. Notice that while one person speaks, the next person gets ready to lob his own comment. He listens only for the lull in the conversation so that he can inject his own brilliant contribution. This is conversation as musical chairs.

Every book on how to win friends and influence people mentions the importance of listening well. It's true, of course—listening to others makes you a pleasant companion and a successful salesperson. However, beyond these practical benefits, listening is a matter of integrity. Paying attention is how we pay respect, both to our conversational partner and to the discussion itself.

Good listening is active—not a passive pause in your own running commentary. You're a participant in a conversation, not an audience at a lecture. You need to provide some signals that you're alive and engaged. There are two key ingredients to active listening: (a) asking questions and (b) repeating in your own words what the other person said.

These two procedures are connected: The best way to ask a "listening question" is to reformulate the other person's comment and to inquire whether you understood him correctly.

Paraphrasing the other person's comments is especially useful when you're having an exchange with someone who's more interested in arguing than in having a conversation. He can't play Ping-Pong alone. Your restatement of his view shows that you care about getting the issue right, not just about winning a verbal duel. This approach sometimes shames the other person into paying attention to you when you voice your opinion. Pretty soon, you may actually find yourself having a genuine conversation.

Repeating the other's person argument as clearly as you can is also an effective tool in defusing many personal disputes. By working on understanding each other's point of view, you can help narrow the distance between those views.

Asking questions is not only a wonderful way to learn but also a wonderful way to teach. The great practitioner of this technique was Socrates. Old man Socrates would stop everyone he met in Athens and ask the big philosophical questions. Socrates had his opinions, all right, but they only emerged from his questions. I'm sure lots of Athenians considered him a royal nag, but his Socratic method has become a standard for the teaching profession.

It's My Idea—Mine, Mine, Mine

I have this great idea for a movie. The story is about a hot affair between the First Lady and a male stripper. Can you steal the idea from me, even though you now see it in print? Absolutely. Copyright law grants me ownership of the form or the packaging of the idea, not the idea itself. Had you plagiarized an actual screenplay, you'd be hearing from my lawyer. Ideas may not have legal protection, but in our conversations, we constantly claim ownership of our intellectual properties. We think our ideas belong to us. Even those of us who aren't particularly possessive about our cars, our toys, our men or women, become maddeningly jealous about our opinions.

Howard threw out a comment a minute ago and now is ready to fight to the argumentative death in its defense. It isn't some principle to which he has deep attachment. It's just some passing notion to which he is now indelibly connected. Howard confuses the worth of his argument with his self-worth. As a result, he interprets every attack on it as a personal attack.

Productive discussions are team efforts. In an honest conversation, no one owns any particular idea. Your contribution belongs on the table for everyone to consider. When the exchange is not a battle for supremacy but a shared attempt to achieve clarity, no one cares who said what. Your attitude should be: If my view is wrong, then it's the view that's wrong, not me. Easier said than done, I know. We want and deserve credit for our insights (although we somehow manage to forget to give credit to the editorial or article from which we borrowed our brilliant gem). Don't worry about the impression you're making—that's for later, not during the flush of conversation.

(What do you think of making that male stripper an ex–bond trader? Here's my idea . . .)

Expand Your Repertoire

What's your rap these days? Most of us have one. Is it a disquisition on the stupidity of television, the rapacity of multinational corporations, the overbearing gays, how the Yuppies had it coming to them, the thrills of motorcycling, the perils of tuna fish? Some people are always ready to mount the soapbox. (It's the twelfth time you've heard this guy's tirade and it was already boring the second time around.)

The worst sort of rap is the pet peeve. Pet peeves manage to smuggle their way into every conversation, no matter what the topic. Marty is hung up on America's foolishness in not imposing tariffs against the Japanese. It's not clear why he takes this so personally, but he's definitely obsessed with the problem. The topic of conversation is Monday-night football? Marty contrives a quick segue to the state of television in America, orchestrates a smooth turn to the subject of the future Japanese control of the entertainment business, and—presto—tariffs. Marty's rap is boring for the same reason the preacher's is—it's predictable—but it's also an imposition. He uses friends as a sounding board for his venting.

A word of caution: You may have a pet rap and not be aware of it. We like to think of ourselves as fonts of fresh wisdom, little realizing how we cling to our old scripts. If you ask your friends what your pet rap is, you'll probably be startled by the consensus. They know because they suffer from your spouting. Try to wean yourself from your favorite spiel. Surprise yourself.

Head-Talk Versus Heart-Talk

Most of us fall into one of two categories of conversationalists: those who talk with and to heads, and those who talk with and to hearts. Some of us believe that what is most essential about a person is how he *thinks*. For others, what counts most is how someone *feels*.

Conversations between head-talkers and heart-talkers can be maddening. The first type fixates on the merits of the argument. Is it rational? Is the evidence sufficient? The second type focuses on the psychological context. Why does the person subscribe to the view he advocates? What in her psychological background makes this point of view so appealing to her?

Head-talkers, for whom logical reasoning is paramount, believe heart-talkers are soft-minded. They see them as fuzzy thinkers unable or unwilling to sustain rigorous analysis. Heart-talkers, for whom the emotions are most important, consider head-talkers uptight and detached from their feelings.

We all recognize that if the topic is a logical puzzle, your feelings aren't important, but if your personal interests are at issue, then your feelings matter very much. Most conversations, however, aren't that clearly demarcated. To achieve balance in your conversations, work against the grain of your natural inclination.

Don't Play Psychologist. Catherine is trying to make a point. She's offering a passionate defense of her belief in reincarnation, when instead of dealing with the substance of her argument, you "explain it away" by focusing on her peculiar psychological needs.

This deflection involves the error of reasoning known as "the genetic fallacy": rather than attacking the argument, you demolish the person's motives for supporting it. I tell my son that Lincoln was assassinated and, adoring child that he is, he believes me. We now know why the boy believes that Lincoln was assassinated, but that doesn't determine whether his belief is true or false. A future team of neurophysiologists and psychologists may perhaps be able to explain why we *believe* that $5^2 = 25$, but that isn't mathematics. Sure, we can explain why the ex-smoker thinks it's proper to prohibit visitors from smoking in his house, or why someone in a rotten marriage thinks you should get a divorce. But deciphering why people believe what they do tells us little about the validity of those beliefs.

Psychologizers who insist on focusing on the source of our beliefs have little respect for the force of reason. Obviously, rationality isn't the whole story, but reasoning can and does change people's minds. Not all our beliefs are determined by our childhood traumas.

Don't Rationalize Rationalism, Either. Sticking to the argument is, indeed, an uncommon virtue. But we can get carried away in this direction as well. Behind our heaviest elephant-talk, the most rigorous of conversations, are people. Keep in mind that having a conversation not only advances your knowledge but also satisfies a need for social contact.

You have conversations with people, not idea machines. Even the most abstruse discussion uses the heart as well as the head. Address them both.

Argument: Look Who's Talking

What were the best discussions you ever had? I'll bet they weren't disputes, but conversations in which you and a friend worked out a problem together. Those discussions were open-ended and neither of you was possessive about who said what. No one won those talks; you both did. Conversations between people in agreement are more interesting than conversations between people in disagreement.

Our mothers taught us to be polite to everyone. We somehow got the idea that this means we should also argue with anyone who wants to argue with us. A big mistake.

Don't Argue with Perpetual Arguers. We all stray into verbal duels now and then, but it's not something most of us relish. Perpetual Arguers, on the other hand, live to argue; they're one of the scourges of our conversational life. To the Arguer, all talk is a tennis match and each exchange a rally. An Arguer doesn't care which side he champions. On Monday, Wednesday, and Friday he defends side A; on Tuesday, Thursday, and Saturday, he argues for side B. On Sunday, he argues that it's not worth discussing the issue at all.

Arguers not only love to argue, but they also love to win arguments. They keep meticulous score throughout the dispute and, if necessary, resort to devious rhetorical tricks to ensure their victory. When someone wants to win badly enough, intellectual honesty is an early victim.

Arguers will tell you that the reason they're so contrary is that disagreement makes for more interesting conversation. They also think that their contentiousness makes *them* more interesting. They're dead wrong on both counts. Arguing for the sake of arguing is adolescent, and extremely tiresome. Don't get trapped into arguing with the persistent Arguer. He's not after enlightenment, he's after victory, and you're playing his game. Frustrate the guy—agree with him!

Don't Squander Your Passion. I'm not Irish. The continuing strife in Ireland upsets me, but I must admit that I haven't lost sleep over it. If we took every human tragedy to heart, we'd never sleep. (Those who never take *any* human tragedy to heart don't deserve to sleep.) Now just because I don't torment myself over the issue doesn't mean I don't have opinions about it. For a cup of coffee, I'll be happy to regale you with my solution to the Irish problem. For a second cup, I'll share with you my take on the dilemma in Kashmir and, generous fellow that I am, I'll even throw in my criticism of conceptual art.

I won't, however, deliver my Irish speech to a member of the IRA or to an Irish Protestant. For me, the issue is a subject for speculation; for them it's a matter of life and death. Few issues in this world engage your genuine passion. Casual analysis of those issues by others makes you angry. It's not so much that these people are uninformed as that they don't care. You do.

I follow this rule: I will talk to almost anyone about almost anything, but I won't have serious discussions about an issue over which I lose sleep unless the other person—on my side or opposed to it—also loses sleep over the same issue. (To draw a distant analogy: It's all right to have casual sex with someone who wants casual sex, but it's not all right to have casual sex with someone who approaches the affair as a profound romantic involvement.) Don't squander your passion on the passionless.

The Principle of Falsifiability

You've been advised here not to get into arguments for the sake of arguing and not to argue passionately with people who don't share your fervor over a particular issue. In the real world of conversation, we regularly get trapped in unwanted arguments. How does this happen, and why are these arguments so unproductive?

Perhaps the main reason such discussions founder is that we don't establish criteria for them. The way to avoid getting trapped is to apply the *principle of falsifiability*. First, I'll define the idea in its fancy philosophical garb, but don't get scared off—I'll be back with plain English in a moment. The principle of falsifiability, developed by the philosopher Karl Popper, tells us that a statement of fact (that is, a statement about the world, not a proposition that's true or false by definition or pure deductive logic) is meaningful if, and only if, in principle, it can be disproved.

So much for the jargon. Now for the explanation in simple English. When someone argues a case, he also has to tell you what it would take for him to admit that he's *wrong*—what evidence would blow his position out of the water, or at least weaken it. Because if nothing can *possibly* undermine his view, then he's not arguing his position, he's simply—and dogmatically—asserting it. It becomes a matter of faith, not reason.

Good scientific theories are always falsifiable. The law of gravity states that what goes up must come down, but if objects stayed up, we'd scratch the theory. If you can't be wrong, you can't be right, either.

Let's see how this principle works in everyday conversations and arguments. You've met Martha before. Pleasant woman, but a bit of a space cadet, especially when she's doing her number about astrology. You regard astrology as mild fun at best. Martha, on the other hand, takes it seriously and thinks everyone else should, too. You've discussed this with her before, and here you go again.

Martha is reporting that the horoscope predicted today's news accurately. You gently ask her a few pointed questions. You wonder, for example, why the moon and stars affect personality but not appearance—people with very different physical features are born all over the world at the same time. You also ask why birth is the key moment for astrology, and not conception, when genetic imprinting takes place.

Martha dodges the questions, so you push on. You point out that current astrology charts are based on ancient astronomical data that no longer are valid. You discount the supposed influence of the planets on the newborn by noting that the gravitational pull of Mars on the infant is far weaker than the gravitational pull of the obstetrician. You question why astrological predictions are so vague. You argue that when not vague, the predictions are often wrong—according to his chart, the fellow in the corner is supposed to be focused and structured, but he's frantic and erratic. "Well," Martha answers, repeating the standard line, "the stars don't compel, they impel."

You've heard this before. "How come every time an astrological prediction doesn't pan out, astrologers shift to some free-will defense, implicitly admitting that the stars don't control destiny?" On and on it goes . . . nowhere. Martha sidesteps the barrage of your counterarguments, while you become increasingly exasperated.

Finally, you ask the critical question: "Okay, Martha, I give up. This is going nowhere. What would *you* consider a genuine challenge to your position? What would it take for *you* to admit you're wrong? Because if nothing I could possibly say, no facts or reasons, could get you to yield, then you're not arguing, you're preaching." This is precisely the thing to say—but you should have said it much earlier.

Astrology isn't the issue; I suppose sophisticated practitioners of it have answers to the objections raised above. The issue here is how we argue, how we deal with contrary evidence—or, more precisely, how we refuse to deal with it at all. In the preceding scenario, Martha is the culprit, but we all tend to ignore counterarguments when our own pet theory is on the docket. We present our case as if we're open to challenge and objective analysis, but in truth, we won't retract our opinion, no matter what anyone says. The refusal to allow even the *possibility* of being wrong is what makes many of our conversations so frustrating.

Use the principle of falsifiability in all your discussions. Who's the best shortstop in baseball? Don't bother arguing the matter unless you've first agreed on what defines excellence in a shortstop. If the discussion is about the merits of a particular movie, first establish what qualities make a film worth seeing. If you're debating the morality of homosexuality, first set out what constitutes morality. (A cautionary note: Don't bother to argue with conspiracy theorists. They're totally immune to counterevidence.) No matter what the controversy, you need to *establish criteria of evidence*. If you don't, you'll end up with two monologues instead of a dialogue.

The Closed-System Trap

Even the principle of falsifiability can't always rescue you. When the conversation heads off into ideology the traps are more subtle, and among the most devious is the closed system. Closed systems are so sneaky that sometimes even the perpetrator is unaware of what he's doing. The perpetrator might be you.

A system is closed when it defends itself against challenges by appealing to the truth of the system itself. Here are examples of how these systems operate. Let's begin with a religious argument.

He: "Do you know why you refuse to accept the truth of our religion? Do you know what your problem is? It's pride. Sinful pride. And pride, my friend, is the work of the Devil."

You: "I don't believe in the Devil."

He: "I understand, but that disbelief is itself the work of the Devil. Don't you see how manipulative the Devil can be?"

Perhaps you've had an encounter with the closed system of a sloganeering Freudian.

She: "It's clear you're a passive aggressive. You act kindly but you're really very angry. This kindness is actually repressed hostility seeping out."

You: "Well, I don't feel hostile at all. I don't feel the least

SAVING YOUR BREATH

If you didn't spend your younger years in a coma, you passed many long nights arguing vehemently about religion, politics, and morality. You and your friends tried out different views, often switching positions with one another. Now that you're older, these discussions have become predictable. Everyone knows what everyone is going to say. And yet, you still find yourself caught up in these meandering debates, wasting time and energy.

The principle of falsifiability can rescue these discussions. Here's how it might work when applied to religious arguments; you can use it effectively in political and moral arguments as well.

Say you're having a discussion with a fundamentalist Christian. You ask: "Imagine that we discover intelligent life on Pluto. Imagine, too, that these beings are vastly more intelligent than we are. Suppose, still further, that they're all Hindus. Would that shake up your faith in Christianity?"

"Absolutely not," answers your fundamentalist friend. "IQ is irrelevant." So you try a few other hypotheticals. You ask how she would react if, say, someone discovered compelling evidence that the New Testament was the imaginative creation of a second-century fiction writer.

"It wouldn't make any difference," insists the believer. "My conviction is so certain that no evidence in the world could cause me to reconsider it."

Now let's suppose you're the religious one, arguing with an atheist. You ask: "Imagine that a 'godly' voice in the morning tells you how many times you're going to sneeze in the next five days, and the prediction turns out to be absolutely correct. Would that perturb your atheistic convictions?"

The atheist replies with an emphatic "No." This atheist also insists that you can't possibly produce any evidence that will alter his convictions.

In both cases it's time to roll out the principle of falsifiability. Perhaps brilliant Plutonians or prognosticating voices aren't fatal counterexamples to religious or atheistic views. But *something* has to be. If both sides of a religious argument refuse to allow even the *possibility* of being wrong—as is typical of religious and political arguments—then you're getting statements of faith, not rational discussion. Statements of faith have their place in a dialogue. But they aren't arguments and shouldn't be presented as such.

bit angry. And to tell the truth, I think this psychobabble is a lot of hokum. I don't buy it."

She: "Of course you don't buy it. That's part of your repression. You refuse to come to terms with your anger. Your refusal to accept this analysis only confirms your passive aggression."

Maybe it's true. Perhaps the Devil is tricking you into not believing in the Devil, and perhaps your refusal to accept this psychoanalytic explanation for your behavior is the result of your psychological obtuseness. It's possible, too (to take examples from other closed systems), that your objections to socialism are just another manifestation of your bourgeois thinking, or that your reluctance to reduce everything to a question of physics is itself a manifestation of the interactions of your brain cells. Perhaps, but to prove this, you will require much stronger evidence than the circular reasoning of the closed system.

This depiction is something of a caricature; advocates of the Devil, Freud, Marx, and scientific reductionism are often more sophisticated than those sketched here. But closed systems of this kind are common. Closed systems bring out the worst kind of intellectual dishonesty and smugness. Their advocates behave as if they're open to criticism, but in actual discussion all your objections get sucked into an endless tunnel, and nothing you say makes any impression. Closed systems are both self-fulfilling and self-defeating: Seeking to explain everything, they explain nothing.

5

Emotions

*Tragedy is if I cut my finger; comedy is if you fall into a
manhole and die.* —Mel Brooks

*The world is a comedy to those who think, a tragedy to
those who feel.* —Horace Walpole

F*or the life of me—my friends say the death of me—I'm
not sure why I still live in Manhattan. It's got its attractions, I
suppose, or at least it once did. But one ritual that will never
make it on anyone's list of urban charms is the morning subway
ride.*

*I go down the subway steps to catch my #1 IRT train and
realize that I'm tokenless. Once again, I have forgotten to buy
extras. And once again, I'm running late for my appointment. An
older woman wearing an enormous dirty orange hat and carrying
an even larger and dirtier shopping bag is ahead of me in line.
Perhaps in London they'd call her a "charming eccentric," but*

*here she's just another weirdo. She leans toward the token clerk
as if she were a pitcher getting signals from the catcher, shakes
off his answer, and demands that he tell it to her again.*

*The rest of us in line are getting antsy. "Lady, let's move it,"
I command mentally, afraid to say anything out loud. Fat chance.
The woman opens her purse and meticulously begins piling up
her nickels and dimes. This is exasperating; at this rate we'll be
here all morning. Behind me, a very serious young woman in a
very serious business suit has had enough.*

*"Excuse me, Madam," she says, "but this isn't a flea market.
Some people actually work for a living. Count your change when
it isn't rush hour." The woman in the orange hat responds with
a mumbled crudity. Meanwhile, a train has roared into the station.
We'll never make this train, and if this woman doesn't stop fishing
for coins, we can forget about the next one, too.*

*I entertain thoughts of mild violence. I imagine shoving her
to the side so that we can get on with our day. No doubt the
folks at the back of the line imagine shoving her somewhere else.
Onto the tracks, for example. No one will do anything, of course.
We are, after all, civilized people and these are just the ordinary,
fleeting fantasies of an ordinary morning.*

Should I feel guilty about my passing violent thoughts?
Do they reveal some kind of moral defect on my part? "Of
course not," you reply. "Everyone has moments when he
thinks violent thoughts. Hey, just take a drive in traffic and
count them. It's normal and probably healthy. As long as you
don't act on your fantasies, it's not a moral issue."

There are two major reasons for believing that the emotions are not part of the moral domain. First, it's alleged,

morality comes into play only when people interact with each other. Your private thoughts and feelings are nobody's business but your own. Second, emotions are conceived as things that happen to you, not things over which you have control. Therefore, you can't be held responsible for them.

Both reasons are mistaken. Your emotions do count morally and you do have control over them. Your attitudes and emotions, thoughts and desires, all reveal your ethics. Anyone who spends his days wishing he could inflict horrible tortures on innocent children has a serious moral problem, even if he never carries out his perverted schemes. Character is central to morality, and your emotions are central to your character.

As for the issue of control, you don't "fall" in love as if, when strolling along minding your own business, you suddenly plummeted into some romantic hole. You choose whom you love, as you choose whom you hate, whom you are jealous of, whom you fear, whom you admire. As we shall soon see, if you change the way you look at the world you change your emotions. In other words, you *are* responsible for your emotions.

In our society, the dominant moral injunction is *do* the right thing. As a result we've neglected the importance of *feeling* the right thing. The philosophical literature of the past recognized the pivotal role of the emotions in our everyday morality. We need to reclaim that insight. A look at the seven deadly sins will give us some much-needed perspective as we embark on our excursion into the morality of the emotions.

The Seven Deadly Sins Revisited

Do you remember the seven deadly sins? Here they are:

Pride	Gluttony
Envy	Sloth
Anger	and last but not least
Greed	Lust

Notice something interesting about these sins—they're all emotions! The transgressions aren't killing and stealing and kidnapping and the other multitude of evils a person might *commit,* but sins of *feeling.* The sins of the heart are deemed the deadliest of all.

It's no accident that the vices and virtues of the emotions are what we teach when we teach morality. Except for a few dramatic prohibitions such as "no hitting," we inculcate morality by emphasizing the appropriate emotions. We educate our children to care about the plight of others, to have respect for opposing viewpoints, to admire hard work and accomplishments, to cherish self-confidence. We instruct our children in the appropriate negative emotions, such as outrage at injustice and anger at those who cheat and bully.

The emotions are considered crucial in moral training partly because having the right emotions leads to doing the right thing as a matter of course. What, after all, leads to murder and rape and stealing but the sins of anger, anger mixed with lust, and greed? As important as the fact that emotions lead to consequences in behavior is their ability to reveal our moral character. Consider the following scene:

Sunday afternoon. Jesus Christ is sitting on the living room couch drinking beer. Two middleweights are slugging it out on television. One fighter lands a hard left hook on the other's nose. Jesus jumps up from his seat and yells, "Good hit! Get the bastard!"

An unlikely scene. Jesus hasn't done anything particularly immoral here, but his emotional response doesn't jibe with his moral character. We don't expect Mother Teresa to remain unmoved by the sight of starving children or even to enjoy a bullfight. We expect morally pure people to have morally pure emotions. The rest of us aren't angels, but we aren't devils, either. We have mixed emotions to match. By examining our emotions we can get a clue as to where we fall in the spectrum.

Emotions and Character

It's difficult to determine how we "really" feel about a moral issue when our emotions lead us in one direction and our reasoned judgment takes us in another. Here is Lisa's dilemma:

I recently had a very upsetting and confusing experience. I was talking with my friend Veronica, someone I always considered open-minded and sophisticated. In the course of our conversation, I mentioned that I was a lesbian. It's something I always suspected she suspected, but it was time to get it out in the open. Out of the closet, as they say.

Veronica's reaction absolutely floored me. She was appalled. How could I? It was unnatural, terrible, immoral. Had I thought about therapy? She kept telling me how upsetting it all was, how stunned she was. I must say, I was shocked by her response, and it hurt me deeply.

Five hours later, Veronica called me on the phone, utterly apologetic. She couldn't believe how insensitive she'd been, and she was terribly sorry. Her impulsive reaction was just that—an impulsive reaction—but I should be assured that it wasn't her true attitude. She said she believed my sexual orientation was my own business, and that I should live as I choose. She was sorry for being so emotional. Sorry, sorry, sorry. And she really was. So here's my question: Which is the true Veronica—her reflexive emotional response or her more reflective response five hours later? What shows her true character—her gut feeling, or her considered views and actions?

The correct answer to questions of this kind is rarely either-or. Both Veronica's unfiltered reaction and her thoughtful one reveal her values. It would be nice if we could just sit back, reach rational judgments, and then have the appropriate corresponding emotions. Usually, however, we carry some unresolved conflict within us. Sometimes we manage to control our emotions, sometimes we don't, but in either case we can still wonder what our true beliefs are.

Here's a case where your rational convictions control your emotional tendency. Let's suppose you harbor vague racist sentiments. You experience a slight unease when you're around people of a different skin color, but you don't consider yourself a racist. You emphatically believe that it's ludicrous to judge people on that basis. You acknowledge the bigotry within you, but you deny it credence and act without prejudice. Would it be to fair to call you a racist?

Conversely, here's a case where your emotions win out. You can't stand your boss. Any time he says something negative about your work you feel yourself exploding inside. Some of that visceral response seeps out in your gestures and muttered curses, although you recognize that his comments aren't excessively critical or unfounded and that you're overreacting. Do you *really* believe your boss is giving you a hard time?

There's no clear answer; we react to the world on many different levels. Our morality is determined by how well we orchestrate our conflicting feelings and beliefs. Perhaps we begin with our gut feelings, but we can't remain there. Gut reactions are just that—reactions of the gut, not the head or even the heart.

To see more clearly how emotions manifest our character and why we're responsible for them, let's take a closer look at one of the seven deadly sins.

Green with Envy

Envy is an unappetizing emotion. It stands out from the rest of the deadly sins (and most other emotions) in a number of interesting ways.

Envy doesn't feel good. All of the other deadly sins are sins of pleasure: We enjoy food, sex, vanity, ownership—even anger offers the satisfaction of a revenge fantasy. Each tempts us with its promised delights. Envy, on the other hand, is no temptation. Envy offers no joy. No one relishes the pangs of resentment and inferiority that accompany it. Horace, in the

Epistles, says of envy: "Sicilian tyrants could never have contrived a better torture."

Envy isn't a sin of excess. Another way in which envy differs from its sister sins is that even a little of it is a problem. Gluttony isn't the vice of eating but of eating too much. It's all right to relax; it's laziness that gets you in trouble. It's permissible to covet the right person at the right time, but not the wrong person at the wrong time. You aren't supposed to be greedy, but no one demands that you become an ascetic. When you shouldn't be envious, however, you shouldn't be envious at all.

Envy is humiliating. You may admit to laziness—almost everyone enjoys a weekend of sitting around on the couch flipping through magazines or watching the tube. And while we aren't proud of it, we will admit to losing our temper once in a while. Many of us will even speak with pride about our lust. But we don't acknowledge our envy. We're embarrassed by it. Envy is a demeaning emotion.

Why is envy demeaning? Because it highlights what we want but don't have. Envy shines a spotlight on what we value, and we'd often rather keep those values concealed, even from ourselves. For example, some people go on and on about how they hate parties and complain about how shallow the conversations are at those gatherings. The truth is that they wish they had the skills to socialize more easily at these events and envy those who can. Other people will tell you how much they disdain wealth, how unimportant it is to them, yet they feel intense envy when they drive by mansions or read about the lives of the rich.

It's worth emphasizing, too, that envy can sometimes take the form of admiration of another's positive qualities. Admiration for someone else's success then becomes a strong incentive for our own ambitions. Your admiration of Eric's extraordinary self-discipline gets you to hit the books harder, while your esteem for Meredith's wonderful social skills stimulates you to hone your own conversational style, and your appreciation of Brenda's ability to stick to her diet helps you stay off the blueberry muffins. So, too, your respect for other people's moral commitment can inspire your own moral growth. Typically, though, it's not Eric's work habits we crave but his new Jaguar, not Meredith's charm but the parties she's invited to, not Brenda's self-denial but her terrific figure.

Envy reflects our values by showing us not just what we want, but also what we would do to get what we want. We might envy Eric for his Jag, but we're less likely to envy the mafioso with the stretch limo. Why? Because we're envious only of people who make their money in ways that we condone. You'd be perfectly happy to have orchestrated smart stock investments, or to have won the lottery or discovered some long-lost deed in the attic. You wouldn't be happy (I hope) if you became rich by stealing someone else's money. Gangsters envy successful crooks, but you don't.

We envy people for getting what we want in ways we can imagine. The more distant the possibility of achieving a certain kind of success, the weaker the envy. You probably don't covet the power wielded by the President of the United States, at least not intensely, but the loser in the presidential race does. On the other hand, you might envy those closer to home—for example, the president of your company— because that's not such a stretch.

How can you control your envy? The same way you control all your emotions: by changing your beliefs. Convince yourself—and this is difficult, I know—that your life will not be essentially improved by a new patio, and you'll no longer envy your neighbor's new addition to his house. Give up on the notion that you own your wife's femininity and you won't become "insane with jealousy" when she playfully flirts with other men. When you change your values, you change your emotions.

While this is easier said than done, success depends in part on *understanding* how our evaluations direct our emotions. To gain that understanding, we need to do a bit of philosophical analysis.

Taking Control of Your Emotions

1. Theoretical Underpinnings

What is an emotion? Don't expect quick and easy answer. Some philosophers and psychologists have suggested that the word "emotion" is so hopelessly vague that we should scratch it altogether. What we can do is clarify some of the features that distinguish emotions from other experiences.

Emotions are feelings aimed at targets. I tell you I feel nauseated this morning and you ask me why. I say I'm not sure but maybe it's something I ate. A reasonable answer.

I tell you I am enraged this morning. You ask whom I am angry with and I say I don't have any idea. I'm just infuriated, that's all. This is not a reasonable answer.

Feelings aren't *about* anything. Emotions are *always* about something. If you're angry or in love, then you must be angry or in love with someone; if you're sorry, then you must be sorry about something that happened; if you're afraid, then you must fear something that might happen. Feelings have causes but not objects. Emotions have both.

Emotions require beliefs. Every emotion has a belief that goes along with it. When that belief changes, the emotion changes. Take fear, for example. To be afraid is to believe you're in danger. A lion walks into the room, roars, and shakes its mane. You're terrified. Suddenly the roaring stops and the lion comes to a standstill. It doesn't move at all. It dawns on you that this is a mechanical lion powered by batteries. Poof! The instant you become aware that the lion isn't real, your fear disappears. You no longer believe you're in danger, so you're no longer afraid. The emotion runs in tandem with the belief.

That's how all emotions work. You can't be upset that the home team lost unless you believe that the home team lost, and you can't be in awe of your mentor unless you believe he or she has admirable qualities. How you see the world determines the emotions you experience.

Emotions involve evaluations. Let's fine-tune our definition of emotions even further. You're offended when you feel you've been wronged. Note the value judgment in "wronged." You can't be angry with Mark for not calling the real estate agent this morning if you specifically told him not to. That's contradictory.

When you have an emotion, anger or any other kind, you make a value judgment. You feel remorse for a comment you made this morning because you believe it was a stupid thing for you to say. You feel proud of yourself because you think your accomplishments are worthwhile. Emotions are targeted feelings, based on beliefs and evaluations.

2. Applications

Are your emotions morally justified? *Moral* emotions are composed of *moral* beliefs and *moral* evaluations.

Our emotions are immoral when they are inappropriate in moral contexts. The immorality of the bigot, for example, is that he lets himself see certain people in an irrational way in order to satisfy his own preconceptions. To rid himself of his prejudices, he must learn to see these people in a different way.

Emotions are central to your morality. As we've seen, you can control them and you're responsible for whether you do or don't. When, then, are emotions inappropriate? Here are some questions to ask yourself in making that judgment.

1. *Is this emotion directed at the proper target?* For no apparent reason, God favored Abel's offering more than Cain's. That made Cain mightily jealous of his brother. Cain, no doubt, was angry with God, but there isn't much you can do with anger toward God. So Cain killed his brother, Abel. We are Cain's descendants, and we all have our prejudices. First we "establish" the facts and then we slide into the corresponding emotions. When the "facts" are dishonest, the emotions will be, too.

We treat some people in our lives more leniently than others, always giving them the benefit of the doubt. We want to love one individual, so we attribute to him wonderful qualities—often ones he doesn't possess. Sometimes, on the other hand, we dislike someone, so on the basis of the flimsiest evidence we blame him incessantly. Because emotions require beliefs, we have to convince ourselves that the object of our hatred is guilty as charged. When you despise someone, that's easy to do.

Psychoanalysts speak of transference, the process of exchanging one person for another as the target of your emotions. One ugly kind of transference is scapegoating. Scapegoating is a group emotion. In one all-too-common scenario, a weak group in society is chosen to carry the blame for the multitude of misfortunes suffered by the society at large. The same process of emotional dishonesty is at work. First, new facts are created that are supposed to show just how evil the subgroup is. Then the hatred follows naturally.

Emotions are judgments, and as the arbiter of your own life, you have an obligation to judge fairly. You can bend, of course, and show mercy in one case, toughness in another, but you do have a responsibility to make sure your emotions correspond with reality. Your emotional targets should live in the world, not in your imagination.

2. *Is this emotion proportional to its target?* Melinda is given to overreacting. When you told her she had a run in her pantyhose, she blanched. She said she felt humiliated and dropped what she was doing to run out and buy a new pair. Last week she was ecstatic for hours after you told her she was wearing a lovely sweater. Melinda is a neurotic extreme, but disproportionate emotions are universal. Every day we read about people who shoot their spouses. They offer anger as an excuse and give examples of what upset them. Anger we can understand; murder is something else.

Most of us aren't murderers and hysterics, but we do let our emotions feed on themselves. As punishment should fit a crime, both your positive and your negative emotions should fit their objects. Keep your emotions in proper perspective.

3. *Has this emotion outlived its appropriate life span?* You know people who hold grudges endlessly. Years after the wrong has been done, the offense remains fresh in the victim's mind and he reacts as though it had just taken place. You know people who fall into despair after a serious mishap and never rebound. You also know people who get rejected over and over but insist on continuing their infatuation. Anger, despair, grief, and sometimes even love shouldn't be immortal. There are exceptions, surely. Some wrongs are so egregious that we can never forgive, and some misfortunes so horrendous that we can never stop grieving. But most emotions should dwindle, lest they become obsessions. You are then no longer in control. Let your emotions run their course and die their natural deaths.

4. *Do you need this emotion?* One way we can control our emotions is by preventing them from developing in the first place. Sometimes it's wise to skip a particular emotional response altogether. You don't have to react to everything.

Margaret is an example of someone who won't let any infringement of her rights go unnoticed. "You don't cross me. You treat me fairly, I treat you fairly, but try to pull one on me and watch out. No one messes with me and gets away with it." Margaret's not kidding. Her emotional antennae are always up, and she proudly reacts to every slight. She is what we gently call "oversensitive."

Not every potential emotion deserves to see the light of day. A few examples: You feel an infatuation coming on but you know it will only lead to trouble. Or you're a bit afraid but you realize that if you give in to your fear you'll lose all control of the situation. Or you've been wronged, but if you give your anger free rein, it will explode, to your subsequent regret. Nip these emotions in the bud; emotions in full bloom are much more difficult to control.

5. *Do you need this emotion now?* Remember the old trick of counting to ten before you react in anger? The idea is that emotions may pass if you allow them to. We can't bottle up our genuine emotions permanently—nor, in some cases, should we. Some emotions, however, should be delayed until a more appropriate time.

Think of the couple who fight wherever they are, in restaurants, in cars, at parties. They couldn't care less who hears them. Personal arguments, like very personal displays of affection, are private conversations and exclusionary. Disregarding others is simply rude. Moral sensitivity requires a sensitivity to place and time. We all can maintain that much control.

6. *Is this emotion demeaning?* Our emotional life is a window on what we take seriously. It's also a window on how seriously we take ourselves. We can understand a child's being jealous because another child received a larger piece of birthday cake. It would be absurd, however, for an adult to be jealous in the same situation. Six-year-olds are insulted by the remarks of other six-year-olds; adults aren't supposed to take offense at a child's words.

Notice that on those days when you feel proud of yourself, you can more easily withstand rebuke without getting angry. When your self-worth is high, these petty insults are just not worth getting upset over. If your emotion shames you, there's probably a good reason to squelch it. Respect your dignity.

7. *Are you using this emotion as an excuse?* We often use our temperament as an excuse for our behavior. Consider these widespread excuses:

1. Yes, I shouldn't have said what I did, but you know how jealous I am.
2. Yes, I shouldn't have said what I did, but you know what a temper I have.
3. Yes, I should have answered back, but I'm a coward.

We pin emotional labels on ourselves and then use them to justify our behavior. We defend ourselves by saying, "What else can you expect from me?" Emotions, however, are not excuses. You *choose* to lose your temper *each* time you do. You *choose* to act in a fit of jealousy *each* time you do. While it's undeniably more difficult for some people to govern their tempers or jealous rages than it is for others, everyone can exercise control.

Notice, incidentally, that we don't reject praise by the same appeal that "this is just the way I am." When someone makes a huge sacrifice to help a person in distress, he rarely says, "Hey, I couldn't help it. I'm so compassionate, I had no control over what I did. I don't deserve any credit."

We used to distinguish ourselves from animals by stating that only human beings can reason. Now we distinguish ourselves from robots by claiming that only humans have emotions. Both assertions are correct. Reason and emotions are essential elements of our makeup. A full moral life incorporates both heart and mind, and we're all responsible for ensuring that we heed the dictates of each.

PART III

The Morality of Making Judgments

Making Judgments:
An Introductory Comment

People judge. They judge people they read about and people they know intimately. They judge issues that matter little to them and issues that concern them directly. They also judge themselves.

We make value judgments incessantly. We choose one car over another, one vacation spot over another, one career over another, one relationship over another. In choosing, we demonstrate that we value one option over the other. So, too, we value one way to live, one code of ethics, over another. But we're often reluctant to make moral judgments. We don't want to be judgmental. It's a pointless fear—in real life you can't avoid putting your values on the line. *The notion that you shouldn't make value judgments is itself a value judgment.* The critical question is how to make those decisions intelligently. That's the subject of the next three chapters.

One of the main hurdles in making intelligent moral judgments is the tendency to make them out of ignorance. Later in these chapters I discuss the need for an "ethics of belief"—the necessity for moral guidelines that tell us when it is appropriate to express an opinion. Sometimes we have no moral right to judge; sometimes we have no moral right not to.

Another hurdle is the temptation to impose your beliefs on others. Imposing your views is usually inappropriate, but other forms of persuasion might not be. With friends, talk is the preferred method of persuasion; with strangers, often the best you can do is be silent. How should you deal with people whose values are, you believe, awry? That, too, is a crucial moral judgment. Expressing your convictions takes courage, but so does admitting to yourself your true convictions. We have to work hard at achieving intellectual honesty. As we shall see, there are traps all along the way.

The following chapters are divided into three categories: judgments of yourself, judgments of others, and judgments of the issues. This classification is not rigid; every judgment involves all three categories. When you judge yourself, your judgments of other people are never too distant. When you judge another person, you base your judgment on your own moral perspective. Before you judge an issue, you always need to canvass your prejudices.

Each chapter begins with a philosophical overview of the respective category of judgment and then points out some of the pitfalls in the way of making those judgments. Each chapter also includes a discussion of how to apply these insights to your everyday life.

6

Judging Yourself

Experience is the name everyone gives to their mistakes.
—Oscar Wilde

Do you have an alter ego who constantly observes you as you go about your life, or do you just carry on your daily activities without engaging in much self-assessment? Most of us do judge ourselves now and again, but our judgments tend to be unfair and capricious. We give ourselves grief over minor personality quirks while ignoring the serious moral flaws that deserve our attention.

How should you judge yourself? Why is moral introspection so darned difficult?

Stop Squeezing Every Pimple on Your Personality

As an adult living in the contemporary Western world, you're suffering from a mental problem that began sometime near the beginning of the twentieth century. The condition began with psychoanalysis and continued with the myriad therapies that have emerged in its wake. We've all become psychologized. The success of Freud's method is a matter of controversy; some practitioners are wonderful healers, while others are disasters. One indisputable result of Freud's innovative insights, together with the contributions of his students, detractors, and competitors, is that we now constantly think in psychological terms. We look for an ulterior motive in everything we do. We search for psychological agendas in every movie we see, every novel we read, and every conversation we engage in. Many of us decide that we're cut off from our true feelings and run for help to the vast psychology mall at our disposal. Here we shop for traditional therapies, self-help therapies, pop therapies, cult therapies—it's a buyer's market.

Our culture has been called the culture of narcissism. What this usually brings to mind is people at health clubs faithfully toning their bodies or fashion vultures hunting for the latest styles at trendy boutiques. But while the fads of body narcissism come and go, psychological narcissism endures. The psychological narcissist is forever polishing her emotional life. She obsessively scrutinizes her personality, searching for defects, agonizing over each imperfection. Encouraged by the therapy industry, she monitors her life with indefatigable devotion.

The psychological narcissist is badly in need of perspective. Her desire for self-awareness is laudable, but she gets carried away. Sure, her personality has imperfections; that goes with being human. Not all the blemishes on her skin are disfiguring and most of her psychological flaws won't get in the way of her life. Perpetually worrying about them will.

We spend much more time tending to the quality of our emotional lives than to the quality of our moral lives. Many people are prepared to shake up their lives in a mad bid for "emotional happiness," but few will disturb their moral suppositions. When was the last time you asked yourself hard questions about your values? Have they changed at all in the last five years? Ten years? Is the way you live in sync with your values?

Before we begin our examination of the process of moral self-judgment, we should contrast it with the psychological introspection with which we're more familiar.

1. *Moral self-evaluation is worthwhile for its own sake.* Want to be happier in five easy steps? Psychology self-help manuals offer the recurrent come-on: You can become happy and you'll find out how in these pages. These books promise to improve your life by showing you how to become more aggressive, solidify your relationships, become a better parent, spouse, and lover, a tougher businessperson. You have a problem? They have the solution.

The desire to change your behavior isn't the only worthwhile reason to undergo moral self-examination. It isn't an exercise in moral therapy. Self-judgment is important because your values define who you are in this world. You want to become acquainted with that person. Be prepared for some surprises, both pleasant and unpleasant.

2. *Moral introspection has results.* Moral introspection is worthwhile for its own sake, but, in fact, it can effect change. A decision, no matter how serious, to alter your personality isn't enough in itself to bring about real change. But once you're acquainted with your values, you *can* succeed in al-

tering them. Simply by choosing to, you can change your attitude toward your friends, your spouse, your lover, the government, and the environment. You are responsible for your choices.

3. *Moral introspection puts you in touch with the big picture.* Doctors study and treat the diseased, not the healthy. Standard twentieth-century clinical psychology emulates the medical model and focuses on mental affliction, on neurosis and psychosis. What it has to say about mental health is only an afterthought. Within this framework, psychological health is the absence of infirmity. This approach won't do for values. As we shall see, a healthy value system isn't just the absence of moral evil. You need to see your life in a larger context.

You Are Your Convictions

Iphigenia, a fictional character living in Athens around 200 B.C., has odd beliefs about herself. She is convinced that she cuts the most dashing figure in Athens, but no one even notices her. She believes she sings beautifully, but no one else thinks she can carry a tune. She considers herself a passionate lover, but the few sexual partners she's had judged her frigid. Her own self-assessment notwithstanding, we can say with assurance that Iphigenia is not debonair, does not have a voice for the ages, and is not a seductive temptress. With regard to these sorts of traits, she's what others judge her to be.

Iphigenia also has unusual moral beliefs. She believes, for example, that slavery is immoral. Now, this is a very strange notion for an Athenian to have at this time. Even the great philosophers of prior generations, Socrates, Plato, and Aristotle, accepted slavery as a natural phenomenon. Iphigenia has other, even more peculiar beliefs. She advocates the strange idea that women should be allowed to own property and vote. Outrageous!

Iphigenia's world considers her moral views eccentric. Today, we think her moral stance makes more sense than her compatriots' morality. Whether you agree with Iphigenia or not, the validity of her moral assessments, unlike her assessment of her other talents, doesn't depend on the support of her fellow citizens. They could all be wrong, and she right. Her values belong to her and to no one else.

Your values, too, exist independently of the judgments of other people. But just about every other trait is defined by the evaluation of others. Consider your physical features. Do you really know what you look like? Suppose you passed yourself on the street and this "other you" were dressed in clothes you don't usually wear. Would you recognize yourself? Maybe not. You've never seen yourself walking down the street, or from fifteen feet away or from behind. (Recall your astonishment when you first heard yourself on tape. "That's me? I sound like that?!" Yes, you sound like that—no one else has difficulty recognizing your voice.) It's a striking feature of our lives that other people know how we look better than we do ourselves.

Assessment of your nonphysical characteristics also depends on other people. You can't be bright or stupid, charming or dull, if you are the only person in the world. Smart compared to whom? A giraffe? These evaluations are *comparative*. The existence of other people also makes it possible to experience many of your emotions—without others around, you'd never feel envious, humiliated, hateful, or seductive.

But your values are different. In the realm of morality, you can be right and everyone else wrong . . . or vice versa. In the domain of your values, you reign supreme—no one else decides your values for you. To the extent that you're in control of your values, you're in control of your life.

Some people walk into a party and you know immediately that you can't mess with their self-definition. You may like them or not, but they are what they are. What does the self-defined person have that others lack? It's not charm, social skill, or confidence. It's self-respect. The self-defined individual has, and knows she has, a solid core of values.

Moral self-definition is strength of character. Think of the wealthy man who has oodles of money, cars, houses, and women but can't feel relaxed with all his goodies. He's never figured out what all this stuff has to do with living the sort of life he thinks he values. Strip him of his toys and he's naked—and knows it. As a result, he exudes weakness rather than success. To the degree that a person doesn't define himself with regard to his core values, others will do the defining for him. He will become a target of their compassion or hostility, an embodiment of rectitude or villainy, an example of values they admire or despise. He will become what they want him to become.

Because your values depend, finally, on you and no one else, you are more responsible for them than for any of your other characteristics. Are you in control of your values? It's tempting to think so, but, as we shall see, it's also easy to fool yourself.

On Moral Nonconformity

No one likes to think of himself as a moral chameleon. On the contrary, we think of ourselves as freewheeling, independent spirits whose moral decisions result from our personal deliberations. This self-flattery is usually undeserved. Moral nonconformity is rare.

A nonconformist is not simply someone who does things differently from the crowd. Lots of people assiduously keep abreast of the latest trends so that they can avoid being like everyone else. A true nonconformist is *indifferent* to popular taste: He is determined neither to comply with nor to deviate from current styles. If it satisfies his inclinations, he will eat in trendy Japanese restaurants, join a health club, vacation at Club Med, and wear a Walkman while jogging around the park; that others do the same is not an argument either for or against an activity. The very term "nonconformist" is a matter of no importance to him since it's a value judgment imposed by other people.

Moral nonconformity is even more difficult than social nonconformity. "The courage of your convictions" is no idle phrase. We live our lives within a changing moral climate, and the temptation to adapt can be overwhelming. Sometimes, just to assert our independence, we stubbornly resist new developments even when we acknowledge their superiority. The moral nonconformist, however, pays little attention to the popularity or unpopularity of his moral positions. He is—it's embarrassing to talk this way in our cynical world—after truth, not applause. Genuine moral nonconformity is difficult to achieve and difficult to maintain. Don't be too quick to assume you're already there.

Moral Consistency Isn't Moral Wisdom

I recently read about a woman who goes to no movie other than *Gone With the Wind*. She said she loves the film and sees no reason to take a chance on a different one. More common is the fellow who only buys Chevys because he's always bought Chevys. And even more ordinary are the people who repeat the same moral point of view decade after decade with the tired explanation that this is what they've always believed and they sure aren't going to change now.

One reason we feel content to stick with our old ideas is that at some point we're bound to be vindicated. For the past twenty years, Jonathan has predicted the imminent collapse of communism. A few years ago, his prediction panned out, and you can imagine his glee. "I called it, didn't I?" he repeats *ad nauseam*. "*Now* you all agree, but I've been saying this for years." But that's precisely the point: He's been making the same claim for decades, so it's not surprising that he might be right eventually, much as a broken clock is correct twice a day. If you mark the same letter throughout a multiple-choice test you'll get a few answers right. You'll also flunk the exam.

As you grow older you notice that even the quaintest notion has its fifteen minutes of acceptability. Moral fashions change like any other, and most plausible moral beliefs will have their day. Holding the same moral outlook all your life proves your stamina, not your wisdom.

Consistency has been called the hobgoblin of little minds and the last refuge of the unimaginative. Perhaps the chief appeal of consistency is that it saves labor. You don't need to rethink an issue as it emerges—all you need is a good enough memory to recall how you felt about it last year. This is not an appeal for fickleness. We all know what it's like to deal with the morally wishy-washy. One day they're socialists, the next day they're capitalists; one day they decry discrimination against those with AIDS, the next day they favor quarantining the diseased. Vacillators have no moral core, but those who are consistent for the sake of consistency have a core that's petrified. Changing your moral beliefs with fluctuations in the weather is ludicrous, but so is etching them in stone. The world grows, and so should your moral views. By themselves, new facts won't force you to change your morality because you can always reinterpret those facts in a way that leaves your beliefs intact. It takes moral courage to change your mind. You want your values to belong to you, not to other people, and you want them to belong to who you are now rather than to who you used to be.

Self-deception and Its Cures

Plato claimed that without rationalization no person could ever do anything he believed was wrong. He thought it a contradiction to say, "I believe this is an immoral thing to do, but I will do it anyway." Surely, however, we do commit acts against our better judgment. The Greek philosophers called these end runs around our principles *akrasia*, or weakness of the will. We backslide, we submit to temptation, and we excuse ourselves through a complex process of self-deception.

Suppose you were asked to list one hundred of your physical attributes, talents, and personality traits and then measured your assessments against some external, objective standard (or as close to objective as possible). You could expect to find many discrepancies between your evaluations and those of the external standard. Some of those differences might be attributable to sheer ignorance—you aren't aware, for example, that your hair is as gray as it is, or that people consider you a classy dresser. Other discrepancies, howevers might result from willful self-deception. You describe yourself as neat when others call you compulsive. This isn't an innocent mistake on your part, because on some level you know they're right.

We fool ourselves not only about our physical and personality traits but also about our values. We assert that we hold to a particular moral principle but our behavior proves otherwise. Consider my friend Scott. He insists that he isn't materialistic. He sees himself as an intellectual, a man committed to ideas and the pursuit of knowledge. Although he mocks faddists and trendmongers, Scott is, in fact, one of them. He hasn't read a serious book in years and gets excited only when the conversation turns to food and vacation resorts. Scott lies to himself about his true interests.

Another friend, Fay, will tell you that the problem with her career is her lack of ambition. Why isn't she more aggressive? Because she thinks it's the wrong way to deal with other people. We need more gentleness, she says. Fine, except that Fay is the most ambitious woman I know. If anything stands in the way of her success it's the enmity she's invited in her unscrupulous climb to the top. Discovering your true moral values takes sustained courage and a lot of insight. Your friends can help here. Find a nonthreatening way to ask them whether your self-image squares with their perceptions.

Moral Guilt

You can also gain insights into your values by considering what makes you feel guilty and what makes you feel proud. Guilt has a bad rap. We consider it excess emotional baggage. We're told repeatedly: If you've got guilt, get rid of it. Too easily said, too easily done. Guilt is a vital moral response to transgression. One important feature of guilt is that it occurs only in those who adhere to a moral code. Perhaps the most frightening characteristic of Nazi commandants at concentration camps was their lack of guilt. Their diaries freeze our blood. In cold, impassive tones, they recount the morning's work of gassing thousands of children, and not until the entry turns to the afternoon's lunch does the writer show any emotion. No moral conscience, no guilty conscience. Should a murderer feel guilty for his deed? Damn straight he should. The person who acknowledges his wrong is a cut above the person who doesn't. Guilt, like punishment, must fit the crime, but some degree of guilt is the appropriate reaction to all moral wrongdoing.

Another important feature of guilt is that it occurs only when we violate our own standards, not those of other people. You make demands of yourself all the time. Ten minutes on the step machine every morning. Don't eat that piece of cake. Don't have that drink. Don't come on to that woman. When we fail to live up to our standards we respond with verbal self-abuse and calls for self-punishment. "What a weak-willed piece of Jell-O I am. I could kick myself."

Finally, we feel guilty only when we violate moral rules that have been incorporated into our hearts rather than just our minds. Most people who cheat on their income tax returns admit that it's wrong, but few are contrite over their dishonesty. Contrast this with, say, masturbation. Almost no one these days considers masturbation a sin—even parochial-school teachers hem and haw apologetically when they teach the profanity of *self-abuse*. Nevertheless, men and women still acknowledge uncomfortable twinges of guilt when they masturbate. The difference is this: You only admit the wrong of cheating on your income tax in theory, but you feel the wrongfulness of masturbation in your primordial conscience. Your moral goal should be to align your visceral morality with your intellectual morality. Guilt is appropriate only for behavior whose wrongfulness you understand. *Moral growth is closing the gap between the values in your head and the values in your gut.*

Guilt is not an all-or-nothing proposition. Only the perfectly sinless can be perfectly guiltless. Guilt, like other emotions, comes in degrees; you can be very angry or mildly angry, intensely jealous or slightly jealous, deeply guilty or just a little guilty. How guilty you should feel depends, reasonably enough, on what you did. A murderer should feel a lot more guilty than someone who cuts into the line at the theater. Line-cutting isn't nice, but you shouldn't ruin your life by tormenting yourself over it.

How do we get rid of guilt? We begin with confession. In the old days, people confessed their sins to God or to a priest. Nowadays, people turn to therapists, who remind them that there can be no cure without self-awareness. It makes no difference to whom you confess as long as your repentance includes self-confession. That's why guilt is so vital to a full

TWO VERSIONS OF ONE-UPMANSHIP:
1. Yes, you're a great scholar. But I'm an even greater scholar.
2. I know nothing. But you know even less.

moral life. It brings our behavior right up against our true values, not the values we think we should have.

The reasons for forgiving yourself are similar to the reasons for forgiving other people. You resent it when people wrong you, and, as I noted earlier, you forgive by overcoming that resentment. Similarly, overcoming guilt is not forgetting what you did but overcoming the resentment you feel toward yourself. We forgive other people for their routine infractions—we all falter. Forgive yourself, as well, for your infractions. We forgive others if, but only if, they admit they did wrong. Similarly, we need to suffer the humiliation of guilt before we're ready to forgive ourselves. We forgive our friends for old times' sake. We forgive those who have acted out of character. So, too, forgive yourself when what you did is atypical of you. Forgive yourself, yes, but not too hastily. To forgive yourself too easily is to destroy your self-esteem.

Moral Pride

Pride is the flip side of guilt. Pride, like guilt, provides a clue to your values; what makes you proud is what you care about. But pride is a morally peculiar emotion. Is it a vice or a virtue? Our moral tradition sends us in both directions:

1. Be proud! No false modesty. Take credit for your success. Stand tall and take pride in who you are.
2. Be modest! Avoid haughtiness. Pride caused the downfall of the angels, and hubris is our constant enemy as well. Pride is one of the seven deadly sins.

We reconcile these apparently contradictory commands by distinguishing between pride and boasting. We're expected to take pride in our accomplishments, but we're also expected not to flaunt that pride by bragging about our victories. The strutting and gloating, not the pride, are objectionable. We're also warned against considering ourselves better than others. But what if you are? What if you do have a better moral character than most—is it wrong for you to be proud of that? Slow down, you say. Talk of arrogance! Who's to say that one person is better than another? After all, we have objective ways of measuring talents, and even then people continually fool themselves about their skills; when it comes to judging values, self-deception is even easier. Doesn't everyone think his ethics are superior to the ethics of others? In fact, no. Many people admit they don't excel in moral character. We may be created morally equal, but we don't remain that way for long. We respect other people for their morality. Why can't we, with due caution, respect ourselves?

Genuine pride is not vanity. The difference between these two emotions turns on the understanding I've been highlighting throughout this chapter. Vanity is about ranking. The vain individual doesn't care about achievement itself but about being better than everyone else. He depends on the applause of others, for without other people his wonderful attributes disappear. He's vain about his looks, his money, his relationships, his talents—all features that provoke envy. Pride in your morality, on the other hand, doesn't depend on the adulation of others. You can be proud and humble at the same time. Genuine moral pride actually requires humility.

Albert Einstein was almost as well known for his humility as for his scientific genius. He certainly realized that he was considered the foremost physicist of his generation, but this comparative judgment meant little to him. He always said that his personal challenge was to understand how the universe worked, and against *that* standard, he barely made a dent. Against that standard he felt humbled.

The question to ask yourself is: What standard of excellence do you measure yourself against? You may be a better person than those around you, but those around you may be moral losers. A moral failure anywhere else is a saint in Sodom. If you believe you've gone far in developing your moral character, you deserve to be proud of yourself. But your moral barometer should not be the values of others but the best person you can be. Who on this earth is as good as that?

THE VALUE OF YOUR LAUGHS AND CURSES

Do you have a good sense of humor? Sure you do. Do you know anyone who thinks he doesn't? A better question is what do you find funny? Do you get a kick out of slapstick? Enjoy jokes about farting? Helen Keller or dead-baby jokes? Racist and ethnic humor? What we find funny is what makes us anxious. Humor is one way we tame our anxieties and make them manageable. That's why we're amused more by the antics of chimpanzees than by those of chipmunks. Dressed-up chimps act so much like us they make us nervous . . . so they make us laugh. Children uneasy about their toilet training think "caca-doodoo" jokes are hilarious. So do adults who still have repressed problems tied to defecation. Those emotionally attuned to physical violence revel in slapstick humor, the nastier the better. Others mischievously repeat cruel jokes that prey on the weak and unfortunate.

Our society's major repression is sex. Consequently, the most common adult joke is the sexual one. Flip through any issue of *Playboy*, past the page where the centerfold shares her profound philosophy of life, and have a look at "Playboy Party Jokes." All the jokes have the same structure. The punch line is a double entendre, a pun with an ordinary meaning and a sexual one. This is the basic pattern of all sexual jokes.

Like humor, cursing has its roots in anxiety. Where sex is repressed, swear words will be sexual. When we castigate others, we use words for genitals. We don't call those we dislike earlobes, nostrils, or good-for-nothing kneecaps. Notice, too, that we use the same expression for inflicting hurt as we do for making love, *i.e.*, getting screwed.

Just as humor and cursing are excellent areas of exploration for psychologists, sociologists, and anthropologists, you can use the same approach to discover your own anxieties. Ask yourself why you find some comic routines amusing but not others. How do you swear? An honest look at your sense of humor and your choice of expletives will disclose much about your fears and anxieties. It will tell you much about your values as well.

Getting Distance

Moral self-judgment is paradoxical. How can someone use his morality to judge his own morality? That's like measuring a ruler with itself! True, we can't get an objective view of ourselves, but we can get a better view than we have now. For that, we need distance. We need to see ourselves, as much as possible, from the outside. When we do acquire that perspective, we begin to see the absurdity of our lives. A little perspective enables us to perceive the degree to which our emotional reactions to the world are independent of the gravity of our problems. The sixteenth-century philosopher Blaise

Pascal noted, "A trifle consoles us because a trifle upsets us." We are genuinely upset about that car accident in which our friend was killed, but we're also upset when the wallpaper hanger is late. The tiny, endless, nagging hassles of each day are the drama of our lives.

Seeing this absurdity won't get rid of your irritation, but it will make it easier to laugh at yourself. As one enlightened fellow put it: "I'm much too serious to take myself seriously." Not surprisingly, our greatest thinkers—Shakespeare, Goethe, Einstein, Freud, and Russell among them—all had a keen sense of humor about our all-too-human affections and vexations. They understood that good talkers know how to laugh, good lovers know how to laugh, and, indeed, good people know how to laugh. Particularly at themselves.

Go Easy on Yourself

You'll notice when your morality is no longer working for you. Your values no longer fit your hopes. You also find yourself feeling guilty, restless, and anxious about your convictions. You're less likely to notice, however, when your morality is doing fine. As with all good things in our lives, we need to take the time to give ourselves credit for our accomplishments, and that includes our moral accomplishments.

Why don't we notice the good stuff in our lives? Because good things don't happen. The good things in life are continuing states of affairs, not events. In the next five minutes countless bad things could happen to you. You could fall and fracture your shoulder, your ankle, your hip. Your dear aunt Christina could break her shoulder, ankle, or hip. The light fixture above you could explode and send glass into your eye. You could get a menacing call from the IRS. With a minimum

JUDGING YOUR WHOLE LIFE

According to some philosophers, if we were truly objective we would accord each minute of our lives— past, present, and future—equal value. In actuality, we accord far more weight to the immediate future than to the past. Interestingly, we do have this objectivity when it comes to other people's lives. The philosopher Derek Parfit explores this deeply ingrained irrationality, and the following "thought experiment" derives from his work.

Case A. You wake up in a hospital bed. The doctor informs you that you have just had a four-hour operation. The surgeons were not able to use anesthesia and you were in excruciating pain. But the operation is over and there are no postoperative side effects. You will have no recollection of the procedure because you were given a pill that expunged the memory of the operation forever.

Case B. The doctor informs you that you will have to undergo an operation one hour from now. The procedure will last only ten minutes but it will be very painful; you will not be anesthetized. Here, too, the operation will not have any enduring side effects and you will be given a pill that will eliminate your memory of it.

Most people quickly say they prefer Case A to Case B. Even though the pain in Case A is much more prolonged than the pain in Case B, it makes all the difference that the suffering in Case A is over while the suffering in Case B is still to come.

Now consider two scenarios involving the pain of someone else. Your mother, for example. You've been on a desert island for three years. Today your rescue boat arrives and you inquire about the health of your loved ones.

Case A. You are told that just yesterday your mother underwent an excruciating operation. The operation lasted for four hours and no anesthesia was administered. A pill was given to her at the end of the operation and she has no recollection of the operation. The procedure has no lasting side effects.

Case B. Your mother will undergo a painful operation in an hour, but the operation will last only ten minutes. Same deal—at the end of the procedure, she will be given a pill that will remove the memory of it, and the operation will have no side effects.

Which would you prefer? Without hesitation, most people opt for Case B. In that case your mother suffers for only ten minutes, but in the other she suffers for four hours. When we think about the pain of other people, future and past are not decisive—we opt for less pain. But when it comes to our own pain, mild or intense, it matters very much whether it's past or still to come.

Is this unreasonable? Are those philosophers correct who conclude that we're profoundly irrational in the way we judge our lives?

of effort you can come up with an infinite number of unhappy events that could befall you.

What good things could happen to you in the next five minutes? Not much comes readily to mind. You might win the lottery, but then there's no drawing today, and anyway you didn't buy a ticket. You might find a hundred-dollar bill under your seat. Peace might break out in the world. But there aren't many more obvious candidates, especially as compared to all the bad stuff that could happen.

This asymmetry between bad events and good events has its basis in the second law of thermodynamics (the law of entropy). This law of physics states that there are always more ways to impair a working system than to improve it. (Thus the wise dictum: "If it ain't broke, don't fix it.") The principle describes molecular structures, but it also applies to daily life. A thriving relationship can come to a sudden and dramatic end—for example, one of the partners can have a fatal heart attack—but flourishing relationships don't flourish abruptly. Good relationships, like most good things, take time and cultivation, which is why we fail to notice the healthier aspects of our lives. Our attention is drawn to unusual occurrences, and most irregularities are negative. You aren't conscious of your breathing, but you will be if food gets stuck in your throat. A few seconds ago, you blinked and gave it no thought. You would have noticed if a speck had entered your eye.

You need, therefore, to carve out some time to appreciate what's wholesome in your life and the lives of those you care for. Don't take for granted that your body is in decent shape, your mental faculties are functioning, and your senses are operating. Any one of these could go wrong at any time. Appreciate, too, your own moral decency. It's not that common.

7

Judging Others

Morality is simply the attitude we adopt toward people we personally dislike. —Oscar Wilde

How to imagine other people's lives when our own seems scarcely conceivable. —E. M. Cioran

Who Are You to Judge?

Most people don't like the idea of judging other people. The moralistic busybody who pokes her nose into other people's boardrooms, barrooms, and bedrooms is no friend of yours or anyone else's. One reason for this reluctance to judge others is our religious tradition, which posits an infallible Supreme Judge who knows all there is to know about us. Only an omniscient God is in a position to judge; not humans, who never know all the facts. Does this mean we can't ever make moral judgments? Of course not. It's true that we aren't all-knowing, and consequently our verdicts must be tentative and open to revision should new information come our way. But moral judgments, even if they're provisional, are unavoidable if you live with other human beings.

Another reason for our hesitancy about judging others is that it makes us feel like hypocrites. We all live in glass houses. Our motto: "Judge not, lest ye be judged." Well, I have some unsurprising news for you—you *are* judged by others. Not only is it true that other people judge you, but it's also preferable that way! A more accurate maxim would read: "Judge others so that you may be judged."

To Judge Another Is to Respect Another

Imagine a world where your behavior is never evaluated: no one ever praises you, no one ever criticizes you. Whenever you do something wrong, people say, "Ah, you know how she is, you can't really blame her. If you knew about her upbringing, you'd understand." Most people hate to be excused in that dismissive manner. We want people to hold us responsible for what we do, even if that means ticking them off. We would much prefer to have people angry with us than have them pity us.

Strangely, when it comes to criticizing others, we suddenly become very "understanding" and refuse to pronounce judgment. We can be amazingly inventive in thinking up excuses to exonerate others' trespasses. Sometimes we turn sociologist and blame the system, the economy, or the culture. Sometimes we become psychologists and point to mitigating factors like stress and insecurities. Excusing others makes us feel magnanimous and compassionate. These are undeserved emotions, however, for what we're really doing is condescending to people and showing them a lack of respect.

People have a right to be punished. They have a right to be treated like adults, not like children or animals. When you refuse to judge someone, you refuse to take that person seriously. Notice how much less likely we are to withhold our judgments when we want to praise someone. We credit people when they do well and admire those with extraordinary moral qualities. But remember: If you refuse to blame someone on the grounds that he's not responsible for his actions, then you can't praise him, either.

Why Excuses Excuse

Not everyone is responsible for his actions. Some people are so emotionally disturbed that it's senseless to prosecute them criminally or blame them morally for the wrongs they commit. We need to proceed slowly here, though, because even the demented are sometimes responsible for what they do. Moral character—good, bad, or in between—doesn't vanish just because someone is depressed, neurotic, or even deranged. Some mentally ill people are sweet and generous; others are nasty and selfish. When inebriated, Drunk A sings sentimental songs of love and friendship and hugs everyone in sight, while Drunk B bashes chairs over people's heads.

When should we excuse? The answer to the question depends on the answer to a prior philosophical question: Why do excuses excuse? We need to do a bit of philosophical analysis. Excuses are not justifications—the terms have different moral valences. When you justify your behavior you claim that in the prevailing circumstances, you did the right thing; you aren't sorry you did it. I don't have to excuse grabbing my child to move him away from an oncoming truck; I was justified in using force to save his life. On the other hand, when you excuse yourself, you're sorry about what happened and offer an excuse to soften the blame.

When we excuse someone for an action, we place the blame on some cause other than his character. Sure, he rammed the car into the building, but that wasn't the result of his recklessness—the poor guy had a heart attack. "Yes, I did what you say I did," he pleads, "but I'm not the kind of person who drives cars into walls. I couldn't help it." Duress, compulsion, and reasonable ignorance are all excuses because they circumvent personal responsibility. We're inclined to forgive people when they can convince us that what happened was a fluke and that they acted "out of character."

Incidentally, this is an important point to remember when considering the merits of an insanity defense. Psychological problems are good excuses only when you can trace the act in question to the psychological deficiency. If you have a kleptomaniac on trial for arson, his mental problem is irrelevant. The fellow isn't a paradigm of mental health, but his compulsion to steal has nothing to do with setting fires.

Here, then, is the rule on excusing other people: *When judging someone for a particular action, ask yourself whether you, in similar circumstances, would rather be "excused" or held accountable for your behavior.* You'll find yourself less ready to excuse than before. Withholding judgment shouldn't be a casual decision.

Three Common Evasions

Deep-Downing

After the bunch of you have finished thoroughly demolishing one of your acquaintances, someone is sure to add, "But deep down he's really good-natured." I suppose this has been said about every human being who ever did anything wrong. I imagine Stalin's buddies sitting around the table saying: "Yes, Joseph does get carried away at times, but deep down he means well."

Alas, some people don't mean well no matter how far down you dig. They're rotten to the marrow of their bones. To excuse them with some vague reference to their buried kindness is a vacuous dodge. (It's bad to be accused of having a mean streak, but it's even more damning to be described as having a kind streak.) Variations of deep-downing can be found sprinkled throughout pop psychology. For example, it's been said of every self-centered S.O.B. that deep down he's really insecure and suffering from a terrible inferiority complex. Doesn't *anyone* have a genuine superiority complex? Surely someone out there is arrogant through and through.

Deep-down analysis is both too easy and terribly selective. We resort to deep-downing only when we defend our friends. It's not much of a defense for anyone.

"As Long As It Makes Her Happy"

Joanne has moved to a LaLa State of Mind. She's gone New Age in a big way. She's furnished her room with exotic crystals, eats foods with names you can't spell, talks constantly about out-of-body experiences, and smiles angelically at in-

JACOB, A THERAPIST
TO DRUG ADDICTS, TALKS ABOUT EVIL

Jacob has spent the past fifteen years treating hard-core drug addicts at a prominent hospital in New York City. It's a frustrating business. When I ask him if he cures anyone, he responds with a laugh that's closer to a groan.

"Let me explain the cycle," Jacob says. "We treat the drug addict when he comes into the hospital and help him get off the junk. Two days later, I walk past the park and see him buying and selling drugs. Before long, I'll be treating him in the hospital again.

"Do you know why most of these drug addicts come to the hospital? First, the hospital is the safest place in town, and most of these guys are hiding from pushers or customers who are after their skins. In the hospital, they're safely out of reach. The other major reason for coming here is to detox. The addict comes here to clean out his system, because by lowering his tolerance level, he can get high faster and cheaper when he's back on the street."

Jacob lowers his voice. "I'll tell you something I wouldn't dare say at the hospital, certainly not at an official department meeting. Many of these addicts have no interest in getting better. They are ruthless. They steal from their mothers, they mug old women, they kill people for pennies. They don't give other people a second thought. Their first and only thought is to satisfy their own immediate needs.

"I'm the head of the psychology department at this hospital and can parade before you the whole litany of the psychological analysis of addiction and deviance. I can go on and on about sociopathic behavior. Psychology-talk is very rich, but it excludes one important explanation—moral choice. If you want to understand these miserable people and the miserable lives they lead, you need to include moral choice.

"Psychology or no psychology, there are evil people in the world. Believe me, I see them every day."

appropriate moments. Let her be, you say to yourself and to your mutual friends. Joanne is under stress, and this New Age kick has raised her spirits. Hey, it beats Valium. Your attitude is charitable and well-meaning—but it's also condescending. As so often in ethics, the Golden Rule suggests the right approach here: How would you feel if people treated your beliefs as a useful sedative?

To be sure, pretending that something is true when you know it's false can sometimes be helpful. Clyde, a professional baseball player, hits better on the days he wears his tattered red undershirt than on days when he doesn't. Clyde is no fool. He's aware that this is a self-fulfilling prophecy: On the days he wears his special shirt, he feels more sure of himself and, as a result, swings his bat with greater confidence. Is this superstition? Of course it is, but it's not worth risking his batting average to overcome the superstition.

It's one thing to play mind-games with yourself to improve your batting average and quite another to deceive yourself about the basic direction of your life. In our hypothetical case, you think Joanne's devotion to crystals is absurd and makes no sense even for Joanne. Don't patronize her. That it makes her feel better isn't a sufficient reason to compromise her beliefs and standards of truth. Think of it this way: You would try to dissuade Joanne from buying a car that you knew was a lemon. Her attitude toward her life is at least as important as her car. If you think her beliefs are lemons, too, then it's your business to tell her why you think so.

We usually adopt the "whatever makes them happy" attitude to avoid confronting people whose views we think foolish. This smug response is almost always inappropriate, but it's particularly obnoxious when it comes to our friends. If we care about someone, we have to care about their standards as well. There's a political application here as well: When governments decide that the people are better off not knowing the truth, you can begin to hear the frightening voice of dictatorship.

"He May Be Smart, But He's Morally Stupid"

One of the great mysteries of the human condition is how some learned people can be so evil. This glaring incongruity is an old puzzle that has been manifested in our century with renewed poignancy. The Nazis emerged from the most highly developed culture in Europe and sank to the lowest depths of depravity. One did not exclude the other. Societies as a whole can be at once sophisticated and cruel. So can individuals. Scan the roster of mankind's greatest scientists, writers, thinkers, scholars, and artists, the best and the

LEAVING WELL ENOUGH ALONE

Fyodor Dostoyevski in his novel *The Brothers Kara-mazov* presents a powerful and instructive rendition of the patronizing attitude that "whatever makes them happy" is all right. He tells the story of the Grand Inquisitor. The argument goes something like this: Jesus Christ has reappeared and he is furious. He's listened in on the local church services and is outraged at what is being said in his name. What an appalling distortion of his message! Jesus meets with the Grand Inquisitor, the head of the Christian Church, and states his intention to go out among the populace and set the record straight.

"Not so fast," warns the Grand Inquisitor. "No way will I let you do that to these well-meaning people. They've grown up with their version of Christianity, as their parents and parents' parents did before them. Their religious convictions provide meaning in their lives. Think how crushed they'd be if you, Jesus Christ, told them that their beliefs were all wrong. It would be like kicking out the crutches from under a cripple, pulling the life jacket from a drowning man. You would deprive them of all hope. How dare you! Their religious beliefs work for them. Leave them alone."

Do you agree with the Grand Inquisitor?

brightest, and among them you'll find the vile and the vulgar.

Particularly perplexing is the immoral artist. All right, I say, I can understand how you can be a physicist and work for the Devil; you don't need compassion to excel at numbers. Reluctantly, I'll even allow the possibility of an immoral philosopher. We've had our share throughout history. But a malevolent artist? How can the soul that composes sensitive poetry or glorious music espouse bigotry and hatred? It can— the likes of Ezra Pound and Richard Wagner are hardly unique. The harsh lesson is that education isn't a guarantee against immorality and neither is artistic genius. Perhaps we shouldn't expect otherwise, but it's a depressing phenomenon, nonetheless.

Lucid moral thinking requires talent and determination. The immoral intellectual has the necessary talent, as we all do, but lacks the necessary moral determination. Brilliant in his work, he is unintelligent in his morality, and his brilliance renders his ethical obtuseness all the more immoral. You have friends like that, don't you, bright people who advocate the most godawful values and sometimes engage in outright moral chicanery?

What are the reasons for this moral stupidity? One is temptation. Aristotle thought of temptation as a kind of intoxication that clouded judgment. Prejudice, too, is a kind of wish fulfillment that overwhelms intellectual honesty. Yet another reason is sloth: The morally stupid are the morally lazy. You have to work hard at removing the debris of your own preconceptions to see your way clear when dealing with moral dilemmas. Some, perhaps even most, people spend more time thinking about the right color for the bathroom wall than about the right way to conduct their lives.

Moral Projection:
You Believe What You Are

Does your moral philosophy fit your life, or does your life fit your moral philosophy? That is, do you begin with your interests and then justify them with a tailor-made ethics, or do you try to live your life based on your ethical beliefs? A bit of both, of course. But which predominates? If you're like most of us, you begin with your desires and prejudices and then invent a moral philosophy to support them. It's frighteningly easy to fool yourself on this score. The self-deceptions of the psychological egoist and the self-hater provide a lesson for us all.

It's a Jungle Out There:
The Psychological Egoist

You've met him. He's the guy who keeps telling you not to be naïve. Talk of ethics is for sissies and suckers, he warns. Don't be a chump. Everyone is selfish, everyone is out for himself, and if you don't watch out for your own ass, it'll end up in a sling. This tough guy has it all worked out. He imagines himself as one of the few realists on the block. In fact, his bravado is little more than justification for his own selfish pursuits.

You point out to him the obvious cases in which people do help other people: the volunteer who delivers meals-on-wheels, the boy who helps the blind man across the street, the young woman who helps the old woman with her shopping. People sacrifice time and money for other people all the time, don't they? "No, they don't," insists our psychological egoist. "It's all hidden self-interest. The people to whom you refer are acting out of guilt, not kindness. They're just trying to make themselves feel better."

You offer a dramatic example: A live grenade is lobbed into a room and a woman jumps on the bomb, smothers it with her body, gets blown to smithereens, and saves the lives of everyone by sacrificing her own. That hardly sounds selfish. "Still selfish," he says. "Maybe she wanted the appreciative eulogies, maybe she did it out of guilt—but she did it for some reason, right? Whatever the reason, she's doing what she wants and that's selfish."

Zap! We've arrived at the core misconception of the psychological egoist. He equates doing something because you want to do it with selfishness when these terms aren't vaguely synonymous. When you do what you want to do, you act *voluntarily,* not selfishly. Selfishness depends on your motives—*why* do you want to do what you do? Giving up your life so that others may live certainly isn't selfish, and neither is helping someone with her groceries, or returning a lost wallet, or giving directions to a stranger, or helping a stranded driver with a flat tire, or the thousands of other big and small favors we do throughout the day.

So the next time you run into this cocky fellow—and unfortunately you're bound to sooner or later—invoke the principle of falsifiability I discussed earlier. When he insists that we all act only in our self-interest—not that everyone should be selfish, but that everyone *is* selfish—ask him what a non-selfish act would look like. If he tells you it's impossible for anyone ever to act selflessly, then make it clear that he's including selfishness in the definition of the word "act." Not only does he have an inferior morality but he also suffers from an inadequate understanding of the English language.

Tarnishing the Golden Rule: The Self-Hater

Few of us are as blatant as the psychological egoist in transforming our personal desires into an ethical world-view. Nevertheless, it would be simple-minded to disregard the powerful pull of our self-image, good or bad, on our morality. Love your neighbor as you love yourself, says the Old Testament. The same idea is echoed in the Golden Rule. The underlying assumption in both formulations is that you love yourself. What happens if you don't and still want to follow these injunctions? For the self-hater, the results can be disastrous.

The way we treat others always reflects to some extent the way we think of ourselves. Think of those days when you're feeling down on yourself—have you felt much generosity of spirit? What about the days when you really liked yourself? Weren't you much more accommodating and compassionate with others? The same correlation between self-image and behavior exists in all people and is reflected in our daily behavior.

You Can't Read People Like a Book

Any moral judgments of other people must include their self-image, but we delude ourselves when we think that gaining such understanding is easy. It's astounding how many people believe they have this extraordinary gift of perception. You hear it all the time: "I can size up people right away. Three minutes and I'll tell you what they're all about. I can read 'em like an open book."

A series of studies has confirmed that people regularly misread others on the basis of their looks. For example, people with scars on their cheeks are assumed to be violent criminals. Good-looking children are judged to be less naughty than ugly children. Attractive defendants get shorter sentences than ugly ones. The problem with believing that you're one of these speed-readers of character who are immune to stereotypes is that no one will ever be able to prove you wrong. If you decide after three minutes that someone is a jerk and then continue to consider him a jerk forever, how can you tell whether your initial judgment was right? What will prove you wrong?

Do you think people can read *you* like a book? You probably think you're too complex . . . and you're right. So is everyone else. We are all multilayered, psychologically tangled, emotionally intricate beings. The interesting things about people lie below the surface, between the lines. Anyone is demeaned by the suggestion that he can be read, interpreted, and analyzed in a scant few moments. If people are books, they're mysteries.

Judging Others: The Method

How much do you have to know about someone before you can judge him? You remember the old aphorism, "Don't judge a man until you've walked a mile in his moccasins."

How do you walk a mile in someone's moccasins if you've spent your life wearing Bally shoes? And what are you supposed to learn during the journey?

We each have a story, an emotional and philosophical biography that shapes our moral perspective. The mile trek gives you a glimpse of that individual's way of looking at the world. You might discover that the person isn't as bad as you thought, but you also might realize that he's far worse than you imagined. The need to place yourself in another's shoes is obvious, but how do you go about it? Most of the time we have to rely on shrewd guessing. Sometimes, though, we have at our disposal a few shortcuts to understanding other people's moral perspectives.

1. Meeting the Family

If you have the opportunity, meet the person's family. Observing an individual interacting with her parents is *always* an illuminating experience. Now you realize how she got to be so charming or insecure, so composed or perpetually anxious. Now you can trace her mannerisms, her various personality quirks. You can truly appreciate—excuse the expression—where she's coming from. To summarize five hundred volumes of psychoanalytic literature: No matter what our age, we remain our parents' child. The gnarled dynamics of parent-child relationships continue deep into adulthood. When you go home, it's still Daddy and Mommy, and you are the child.

Sibling interactions are enormously instructive as well. These patterns begin early and don't change much throughout adulthood. All siblings have their own power relationships:

One dominates, the other is subservient; one is the adult, the other the child. If you're too close to see it with your own brothers and sisters, think of the relationships between your parents and your uncles and aunts.

Of course, you can't meet everyone's family. As we get older, our lives become increasingly detached from our parents', and eventually we're all orphaned. Meeting someone's family is helpful, but it's neither necessary nor sufficient for understanding that person. To get inside another human being, you need empathy.

2. Emphatic Extrapolation

A. EMOTIONS AND MOODS Diet specialists tell us that we have our own "normal weight." We hover around it for decades, sometimes gaining a few pounds, sometimes losing a few. It's much the same with our temperaments. Our outlook fluctuates in response to what's happening in our lives, but we rarely stray too far from our personality norm. Take boredom, for example. Some people are perpetually bored. As far as these folks are concerned, it's all one big drag and the exuberance of others is naïve and childish. We also all know people who are constantly excited. Their enthusiasm is boundless: From the trivial to the momentous, life for them is an adventure. They consider those who don't share their indiscriminate fervor cynical stick-in-the-muds.

You have days when you fit one or the other of these extremes. When you're feeling buoyant, optimism seems perfectly natural and you can't understand how others—or you on your down days—can be so depressed. Alternatively, when you're in the throes of a spell of pessimism, everything seems cold and sober, and your earlier elation appears jejune and frivolous. Don't let these shifting frames of mind pass unnoticed. The challenge is to extrapolate from your own disposition and moods to those of other people. Your own feelings, after all, differ from others not so much in kind as in duration and degree. Now is when you can imagine what it feels like to live in a state of permanent pessimism or optimism.

Use this approach to plumb the full range of human emotions and attitudes. When you feel sexy and sex charges the air around you, imagine what it's like to feel that way every day. Some people do. When you're feeling unusually inspired or pretty, or especially dull or ugly, think of what it's like to live your whole life with that self-image. When you're angry, think of the inner life of those—and their number is legion—who are angry all the time. It's not as easy as it sounds. You really have to concentrate, but it's well worth the effort. These are your opportunities to gain important insights into the emotions and moods of other people.

B. PHILOSOPHICAL CONVICTIONS Emotions and moods are not the whole story. Philosophical convictions also determine a person's moral life, so before judging someone you also need to climb into his philosophical skin.

Do Amish people react differently to men walking on the moon than do other Americans? Do young girls in the lowest Hindu caste have different kinds of romantic dreams than young girls in West Virginia? Does your married neighbor across the street, the one who sneaks out to the racetrack twice a week, have different beliefs about the obligations of marriage than most other men?

Even the people closest to you have different notions about life than you do. They think differently about social institutions, human nature, family relationships, marriage, friendship, death. Different beliefs translate into different inner lives: different fears, different joys, different aspirations, different disappointments. To understand another's value system you need to see it from the inside. That takes an exercise of the imagination.

Most of us have not been in the thick of war or experienced domestic violence, but we have an inkling of these horrors through our imaginative participation in the fictional worlds of novels, plays, and films. Imagination is crucial to empathy and, therefore, to morality. You flip the pages of a magazine and see a picture of a young girl with a bloated stomach and large black eyes. The copy asks you to imagine her hunger pains, for only then will you be moved to donate to this relief charity. The imaginative adoption of new beliefs won't make your breakfast taste any different. You'll pay your bills with the same scowl. You'll enjoy Mozart as much or as little as before. You will achieve, however, a deeper appreciation of the way other people view their lives, and your judgments will be much richer as a result.

Everyone Is Having a Hard Time

You look out the window and see other people scurrying about their business. Sometimes it seems that their lives are real, whereas yours seems aimless and insubstantial. Everyone else seems driven, caught up in his activities, while you feel detached. You envy others' commitment and wish you had their sense of direction. Rest assured: Everyone feels this way sometimes. "We're all connected," sings a telephone commercial, but the truth is we're all disconnected. All of us are alienated sometimes, and when your neighbor is the one who feels cut off she sees you as the one in control. So when you judge other people, remember one overriding axiom: *Everyone is having a hard time.*

Everyone is insecure. Everyone is hassled. Everyone is tired—we all need more sleep. Everyone wishes he had more courage, more money, and better social skills. Everyone wants more glamour in his life, and we all desperately need more laughter. Few can figure out how they ended up living the life they lead. Don't be misled by flippant talk; it's a battle for everyone.

We all create strategies for dealing with the turbulence of life, some more successfully than others. Give people a break. It's not easy doing a life.

AN EXERCISE IN MORAL IMAGINATION

Can you imagine what it's like to have different religious beliefs than your own? This is your challenge. If you're religious, imagine living your life without a God. To the extent that you can, try to experience the belief that our world is purely physical, without a preordained destination and without cosmic purpose. Alternatively, if you consider yourself an atheist or an agnostic, try to imagine believing in a God who observes, cares about, and directs the world's daily activities. Find out what it's like to have a different "ultimate concern."

The point here is to try on the other's view, not to judge it. When you imagine views that differ from your own, your perspective widens and your judgments become much more substantial. As a bonus, you also understand more about your own faith or lack of it.

8

Judging the Issues

The Background:
Three Confusions About Moral Judgment

Bob, your associate, believes it's okay for him to have an occasional extramarital fling. You disagree. Is it appropriate for you to judge his philandering?

You believe it's wrong to kill animals for their fur, but your friend Jessica loves her mink coat. Is her behavior your moral business? Is it your place to admonish her?

Your sister is dating someone of a different faith. You believe this is wrong; she does not. Moreover, she thinks your feelings on this matter have no relevance. Is she right?

These are the sorts of moral dilemmas you confront in the course of your everyday life. When you read about them they're merely theoretical questions; you can choose not to think about them. When they arise in real life, however, you can't evade them as easily. How you deal with issues reflects your central values. Your choices reveal to you and to the world who you are.

How do you make a moral decision? You can flip a coin. You can go with your immediate feelings or you can give the matter serious thought. Moral reflection is hard work. We'd just as soon avoid it . . . and we usually do. The most common way to avoid thinking morally is to redefine moral judgments as something else. The three most popular evasions are:

- turning morality into matters of taste
- turning moral judgments into social judgments
- turning moral judgments into legal judgments

Before we examine how we can start making more objective, honest moral judgments, we need to clear up these common confusions. They're widespread and powerfully misleading.

Morality Is Not a Matter of Taste

I'm at a friend's house for dinner, and some guest, usually the most obnoxious person at the table, finds out that I teach moral philosophy. Inevitably, he feels obliged to instruct me on the true nature of ethics. "You know," he declares, oozing self-satisfaction, "when all is said and done, morality is only a question of opinion. And no one person's morality is any better, objectively, than anyone else's. Morality is a matter of taste." Ten minutes later he's involved in a heated debate about the moral obligation of employees to blow the whistle on companies that violate government pollution regulations.

Did I miss something? Didn't this fellow insist a few minutes earlier that morality was only a matter of taste? Then why all the shouting? Would anyone spend two hours arguing for the superiority of French vanilla ice cream over chocolate-chip? We don't argue about matters of pure taste (although even in taste, standards count), but we do argue about moral issues. We argue about the big social issues such as abortion, affirmative action, and euthanasia, and we argue about such personal, everyday moral concerns as whether Harry is obligated to spend Thanksgiving at his mother's, or whether you should give birth-control pills to your seventeen-year-old daughter. If moral views were arbitrary inclinations, we wouldn't bother trying to get others to see it our way. We do, though, because we take our moral convictions seriously.

Moral judgments, unlike matters of pure taste, are supported by reason. Suppose I tell you that I oppose abortion because abortion begins with the letter A and I oppose everything that begins with the letter A. This is clearly ridiculous. It follows that if some reasons are ridiculous, others aren't. Our problem is rarely that we don't recognize good reasons when they come our way but that we don't reason more vigorously. We take a minute to think about the moral issue, come up with a point of view, and then spend the rest of our lives defending it. Sometimes we so want the answer to be one way rather than another that we deceive ourselves into thinking reason is on our side.

It's true that reason alone is not enough—moral judgments also require compassion and empathy. But any approach to moral issues that discounts reason is an invitation to danger. A history of atrocity confirms the sad consequences.

Moral Judgments Are Not Social Judgments
New Guinea . . . First they build a shed with enormous logs. Two upright pillars delicately support the entire structure. A girl

adorned with the ornaments of a deity is brought in to lie down beneath the roof of logs. Soon the boys arrive.

About six boys enter the room, one at a time, to the accompaniment of drums and chanting. Each has sexual intercourse with the girl. It is the first sexual experience for both the boys and the girl.

When the last of the boys is in full embrace with the girl, the supports are withdrawn, the logs drop and the couple is crushed to death. The boy and girl are then pulled out from the rubble, roasted, and eaten that very evening.

This is not your typical Saturday night in Wichita, Kansas. Cultural practices that violate our own morality pull us in opposing directions. On the one hand, we recognize that different cultures have different traditions and that our own moral views emerge from our cultural environment. We conclude that just as people from other cultures shouldn't judge our way of life, we shouldn't judge theirs. On the other hand, are we truly willing to forgo all moral judgments of other societies? Does this mean we can't disapprove of apartheid in South Africa because it is the value system accepted by so many Afrikaners? Does it mean we can't condemn the Nazis for shoving babies into gas chambers because the Nazis genuinely believed they should? Does anyone, anywhere, anytime, have the right to torture children? Aren't some practices wrong for all human beings?

How do we solve this dilemma? By distinguishing clearly between *cultural relativism* and *ethical relativism*.

Cultural relativism (as I am using the term) counsels us to respect the traditions of other cultures. No culture can legitimately claim that its customs and traditions are superior to those of any other culture. Ethical relativism disallows cross-cultural judgments about moral practices as well.

People eat monkey brains in Southeast Asia. The procedure goes something like this: A monkey is placed in a vise and someone slices off the top of its skull. The diners then pop the still bubbling brains into their mouths. I'm told it's quite a delicacy. Westerners find the feast revolting, but we can recognize that this repulsion is not a *moral* repulsion. Is it morally worse to eat monkeys than to eat chopped-up cows as Whoppers? Since this isn't a moral difference, the cultural relativist cautions us against condemning the practice—our own cultural behaviors are not a standard by which to judge those of another culture.

According to the ethical relativist, just as we must not judge another culture's customs, we must not judge its ethical beliefs. Ethical relativism is initially an attractive theory, motivated as it is by the laudable desire to tolerate other viewpoints. It's a very popular thesis . . . *and a very wrong thesis.* Precisely because it is so attractive and popular, it's important that we examine why ethical relativism is such a confused idea.

Two hundred years ago, most Americans believed slavery was morally justified. Given his theory, the ethical relativist would have to agree that in those days slavery was morally justified—not just that people *thought* it was morally acceptable but that it *was* morally acceptable. If you lived in America back then and thought slavery was evil, then by the lights of ethical relativism you would have made a moral error. For if good and bad are determined by the dominant beliefs of a society, we can't, without contradiction, ever disagree with our society on any moral issue. Ethical relativism also makes it impossible ever to speak of moral progress. How can one society be "better" than an earlier one? This conclusion is certainly nonsensical.

Furthermore, ethical relativists are vulnerable to charges that they hold a double standard. They seem to have no problem *praising* the moral behavior of other cultures, pointing with admiration, for example, at the respect young people extend to their elders in Asian cultures or the communal spirit of nonindustrial societies. But you can't have it both ways—if you aren't permitted to condemn another society, then you can't praise it, either. Your moral outlook is certainly influenced by the culture in which you're raised, but your moral views are still *your* views. You're responsible for your moral beliefs; you must determine them based on your own standards, not society's. Morality is not a popularity contest.

How do you know when you're dealing with a cultural custom rather than a moral tradition? Is the New Guinean rite discussed above an example of a cultural difference whose value is "relative" and beyond the bounds of judgment, or is it a practice of moral significance that requires moral judgment? Deciding whether a practice is a matter of culture or ethics is often very tough and requires true moral wisdom. Consider these difficult cases in which our answers directly affect our foreign policy:

- Women in Saudi Arabia, Iran, and other traditional Muslim countries can't drive, vote, or eat out alone. The testimony of women is not accepted in Orthodox Jewish courts. In countries where Catholicism dominates public life, contraceptive devices can't be sold legally. Are these religious practices we should respect or violations of human rights we should try to change?

- Should we support the overt assassination of a dictator if we have good reason to believe that the regime that follows will support liberty? Should we actively export democracy?

The way you characterize these dilemmas has immediate consequences. If you determine that these are cultural differences they're not your moral concern, but if you think they're ethical issues you're morally bound to bring about an improvement.

Moral Does Not Mean Legal

Morality isn't a matter of personal taste or social standards. It isn't a matter of the law, either. Law and morality are, of course, connected. We want our laws to reflect our morality. But they're different domains with different agendas, and we shouldn't confuse the two.

I ask a friend what he thinks of some comedian who makes his living by telling ethnic and sexist jokes. My friend answers with a righteous affirmation of the comedian's right to say whatever he wants. My friend is talking law, but he still hasn't answered the question. Let's grant the *legal* right—I want to know what my friend thinks of the comedian's humor. Is the act morally offensive? Should the comedian be ignored? Berated? I'm asking for a moral response to the comedian's act, not a legal gloss on its constitutionality.

Law and morality don't always intersect. Lying is morally wrong, but unless you lie on the witness stand it's not illegal.

Parking in a no-parking zone is illegal, but unless you're putting people's lives in danger, it isn't immoral. Complicated problems often generate both legal and moral issues but require different answers. Before you tackle a moral problem, you need to separate the moral aspect from the social, legal, and factual background. Let's see how the process of moral judgment works.

The Process: Cherish the Controversy

Dateline: Planet Earth. 300,000 B.C. Dusk. Two cavemen sit near a brook as the sun begins to set. They have entered their midlife crisis and have grown philosophical.

Caveman A turns to his friend. "You know, the more I think about it, and I do think more about these things lately, the more convinced I am that this world has a point. I mean, here we are, day after day, chasing animals, chasing women, eating, sleeping, dying. To what purpose? I don't have a clue, but I'm sure there's some explanation for this whole maddening parade. Some Creator put this show in motion and for a reason. Or perhaps this whole world, this whole life, is only an illusion. Whatever it is, there's some answer out there, somewhere."

His friend disagrees. "I, too, have been thinking about the Big Questions of late, but I can't agree with you. Not at all. The more I think about it, the more convinced I am that the world is just what it is. What you see is what you get. All this talk about The Big Answer, the gods, illusion . . . it's just wishful thinking. Thinking born of hope, or perhaps

ABORTION: LEGAL PROBLEM OR MORAL PROBLEM?
For a pointed example of the confusion between legal and moral discourse, look at the asymmetry of the abortion debate.

Your friend Carol calls to tell you she's pregnant. She's thinking of having an abortion. She tells you all the relevant details about her pregnancy and wants to know what you think she should do. You tell her you're pro-choice and she should do what she believes she ought to.

"Thanks for nothing," Carol says. "Of course I'll do what I think is right—I didn't ask you about my legal rights. I want to know what you think about the morality of my having an abortion. Telling me that you're pro-choice doesn't answer that question."

Carol is right. The label "pro-choice" is essentially a legal claim. Its advocates believe that only the woman, not the state, has the right to determine whether or not she should have an abortion. That's why a person can, with consistency, be pro-choice with regard to the legality of abortion but "pro-life" with regard to the morality of abortion. Advocates of the pro-life viewpoint, on the other hand, not only claim that abortions should be illegal but that they are immoral as well.

despair. This is life, my friend, the whole story. There isn't anything else."

Regardless of which view sounds more plausible to you, it's likely that human beings had this kind of exchange as soon as they learned to speak. What's not plausible is that the answers to these central questions are so obvious that reasonable people can't disagree about them. It's shameful that believers in one philosophy call its opponents heretics and kill them for their beliefs while heretics, for their part, regard all believers as fools, unworthy of their respect. We call those who disagree with our own views pigheaded, naïve, and callous, and sometimes they are. But religious, political, and moral issues are complex, and we need to remember that decent and intelligent people can reach different conclusions based on decent and intelligent reasons. That we continue to have these differences is one of the glories of the human race.

In Your Humble Opinion

You're at a gathering and the conversation turns to the video market. Someone is nattering on about his new idea for a children's video, which he is sure will sell a million copies. It so happens that you work in video marketing, in children's video in fact, and this guy doesn't know beans about the subject. You consider telling him that you work in the field and of explaining why his idea can't work. On second thought, you decide to remain silent. Listening to this fellow pontificate makes it clear that nothing you say will shut him up.

Scientists don't usually have this problem because most lay people don't lecture others about technical matters of science. Do you have strong feelings about the future of superstring theory in cosmology? Probably not, unless you're a theoretical physicist working in that particular subspecialty. Are you entitled to an opinion about the subject anyway? Sure, if you're willing to be a jerk. Although in some other areas—ethics and politics among them—we can more easily claim a measure of authority, most of us recognize limitations on our expertise. On a few issues we have convictions, on some we have opinions, and on most we have no strong inclination one way or the other. Opinionated people see no such limitations. They feel compelled to express their viewpoint on every subject that comes their way—ignorance is no impediment. They're proud to be opinionated and see it as a sign of their boldness.

We need an "ethics of belief" that places value on the way we arrive at our opinions. A healthy ethics of belief requires that our judgments be based on sound evidence. Opinionated people have a weak ethics of belief. They make no distinction between a legitimate opinion and an arbitrary opinion; all that matters is that they have an opinion. The problem with opinionated people is that they don't take their own views seriously enough! When we do take our opinions seriously, humility follows. We wouldn't assume that we know as much about a subject as the person who devotes her life to it. Would you argue for your theory about the Aztecs, about whom you know little, with someone who just wrote a book about Aztec civilization? Of course not. Keep in mind, however, that opinions don't gain in value just because an authority has left the room. You may insist that uptown real estate prices have recently fallen, but a realtor working that turf could set you straight about that market. You have an opinion about the best buy these days in Persian rugs, but unless you're in the business, your estimate isn't worth the lint on the rug you're standing on.

The result of our national insistence that "everyone is entitled to his opinion" is a massive inflation of worthless opinions. We begin with the democratic idea that everyone has a right to say his piece and then, fallaciously, conclude that everyone *should* say his piece. Does this mean that you're never supposed to adopt a position or voice an opinion? Of course not. Often we must make a choice and formulate our views on the best evidence available to us at the time. Suppose your mother is dying painfully and you need to decide whether or not to authorize heroic measures to keep her alive. With the clock ticking, you don't have the luxury of ten years of deliberation. You must decide immediately. Under these circumstances, you consider the evidence, evaluate your options, and take action. But when you needn't reach a conclusion and you don't have adequate evidence, hold your peace.

Don't elevate your every whim into a conviction. Having an opinion is one thing, delivering the Ten Commandments is something else. Intellectual honesty demands that unless you're a bona fide expert in the field, a hint of tentativeness should accompany all your views and decisions. Indeed, a hint of uncertainty is appropriate even if you *are* an authority. Here's a simple device to ensure that you have the proper humility when offering your opinion: When you speak, imagine that an expert is sitting right across from you. Now offer that opinion.

Dealing with Fanatics

We need to respect opposing views, but respect has its limits. You can't respect the views of those who don't respect the debate itself. As Eric Hoffer notes: "The fanatic is not really a stickler to principle. He embraces a cause not primarily because of its justice and holiness but because of his desperate need for something to hold on to. Often, indeed, it is his need for passionate attachment which turns every cause he embraces into a holy cause." Because a fanatic believes he already possesses the truth, he sees no reason to pursue the investigation. He cannot be convinced; he can only be converted. If you've had to deal with fanatics, you know how disconcerting they can be. Arguing with a fanatic is especially unsettling when you share the same basic ideology. No matter how religious you both are, he'll complain of your inconsistency and spiritual shortcomings. If you're on the political left, he'll scold you for not being radical enough; if you're on the political right, for not being conservative enough.

So how do you answer fanatics? By asserting your uncertainty. Sure, you share some principles with the fanatic, but you still want to explore other points of view. Unlike the fanatic, you aren't afraid of complexity and difference. The philosopher Immanuel Kant offered an exquisite description of the fanatic's rigidity: "A fanatic is someone who dreams according to principle."

Don't Pigeonhole Yourself

We complain when other people make assumptions about our views. We take great pride in saying, "My views can't be labeled." In fact, we pigeonhole ourselves far more often than others pigeonhole us. We approach the world from fixed principles and when faced with a new problem we run for cover under them. Instead of judging the issue directly, we determine how it fits into our ideological framework. For instance, you read about a new increase in welfare payments to keep pace with the cost of living. Whether you approve or disapprove will probably depend not on the merits of the policy itself but on whether or not you see yourself as politically conservative or liberal. Subliminally, you ask yourself, "How am I supposed to think about this issue?" Your ideological positions determine how you judge most issues: abortion, military intervention, pornography, affirmative action, homosexuality, and so on. Loosen up your presuppositions— your views don't have to come in prepackaged sets. You can be opposed to both sexual permissiveness and a hawkish foreign policy, in favor of legalizing drugs but not flag-burning. It takes conscientious effort, but you can judge each issue on its own merits.

Confront Your Biases

We all have biases. Our prejudices affect not only our views about race, religion, and politics but also how we interpret what happens to us throughout the day.

Tom hates city life. This morning he was stuck in traffic for twenty minutes, which he took as one more piece of evidence that the city has become the pits. Tom interprets anything that goes wrong on the streets as further proof of urban decay.

James thinks Rebecca is sweet but irresponsibly spacey. This morning they were to meet at ten o'clock and it's already ten

OH, HOW WE LOVE TO BE MODERATE

You're no extremist. You're no fanatic. On the contrary, your views reflect a healthy, levelheaded balance. It's easy to portray yourself as a moderate. All you have to do is draw the spectrum so that your own beliefs fall right down the center. Shoot first, then draw the bull's-eye . . . dead center every time. No matter what position you take, however, you're an extremist to someone else.

Suppose you consider yourself a "moderate Republican." To a socialist you're way over to the reactionary right. To a fascist you're a leftist. But even the socialist is way over in right field from the perspective of the Maoist . . . and so on.

Religious assumptions of moderation have the same problem. A Presbyterian may think of herself as a religious moderate as compared to the evangelical fundamentalist on the one hand and the atheist on the other. Both the atheist and the fundamentalist, however, view the Presbyterian as an extremist from their own respective vantage points. Similarly, to those of Victorian sensibilities, your lifestyle is downright Bohemian. To the truly kinky, you're a hopeless square.

"Moderate" is an arbitrary designation without much meaning. It's another label you can do without.

minutes past the hour. Still no sign of Rebecca. She probably has her head in the clouds . . . as usual.

Once you commit yourself to seeing the world a certain way, you're sure to find evidence to confirm your point of view. We conveniently disregard those occurrences that contradict what we want to believe.

I remember someone telling me when I was a kid that black people drove Buicks. I have no idea how this person arrived at this weird idea, but I do recall taking note every time I saw a black person driving a Buick. I never noticed black people driving other cars. This is the central pattern of prejudiced thinking, and its hold on us is more subtle and ingrained than we're willing to admit.

Here are a few examples of the way these biases operate.

THE FLIP-FLOP CRUSADER The deepest animosity flourishes in the soil of former adoration. Former lovers become bitter antagonists—think of the venom in so many divorces—and our erstwhile friends become our most implacable enemies. The stronger the previous attraction, the stronger the present revulsion. Having invested so much positive emotion, we now feel humiliated and betrayed; it's just not possible to be indifferent.

The same emotional about-face occurs when we change our beliefs. Witness the former smoker's holy crusade against tobacco. Ex-liberals are the most rabid critics of liberalism, and religious converts are the most fanatic proselytizers for their newfound faith. The crusader recalls his former beliefs with trepidation and anger: After all, not too long ago he was their captive.

This new and intense antagonism is often wildly inappropriate. Think of those conversations when a friend starts carrying on about some minor point. Why such agitation? The issue is just not worth all that attention. So if you find yourself becoming extraordinarily upset by some issue, take a minute to think about where the anger is coming from. Part of the discomfort might be that you once held a very different view about the matter than you do now. Stick to the objective merits of the case and leave your past behind.

THE PRINCIPLE OF GEOGRAPHIC HATRED People hate their neighbors. Here is a telling story about geographical hatred, the hatred between the Serbs and Croats. One day, Franjo, a Croatian peasant, is working in his field when a voice from heaven calls out to him: "Franjo, you've been a good man. You work hard, you have true faith and integrity. Tell me what you want and you shall have it . . . with one little condition. Whatever I do for you, I will do double for the Serb, Josip, who works the field next to yours." "I see," says Franjo, doffing his cap and scratching his head. "Whatever you do for me, you'll do twice for that Serbian? Very well, then, blind one of my eyes."

Just as countries and communities hate their geographical neighbors, so do people hate their ideological neighbors. Protestant Christians battle with Catholic Christians but neither group worries about the Hindus, while Shi'ite Muslims war with Sunni Muslims and neither group frets about the Buddhists. Orthodox Jews are furious with Reform Jews, and vice versa, but neither denomination cares about the Zoroastrians. In each case, the adjacent groups claim the same prize—the true faith—and both sects ignore distant religions.

Perhaps it's in the nature of human possessiveness to guard jealously what you think is yours (physical or ideological) and to allow the most trivial differences to become major contests. Battling only those directly in front of you, however, is a dangerous strategy. Your true enemy can be far away and out of sight. Save your venom for your genuine adversaries.

PROFESSIONAL BLINDERS   To the man with a hammer, every problem is a nail. We each carry our favorite tool. Some people choose a line of work because they think it's important; others think their work is important because they've chosen it. In either case, there's a powerful temptation to translate every problem into one's own bailiwick. The lawyer sees every problem as a legal issue; the artist concentrates on the aesthetic dimension; the nutritionist thinks it all can be explained by looking at our eating habits. Academics are among the worst culprits. They plow one narrow strip of their field all their lives and insist that everything of importance grows right there in their own patch.

The businessman: *"Let me tell you. No matter what they say, the bottom line is the bottom line. It's all business. I don't care if it's international politics, local government, doctors, the art world . . . it's all about money. I'm not saying it's right or wrong. I'm saying that's how it is."*

The historian: *"You look at today's events as having no history. You think the world started this morning. I have a different perspective. We historians appreciate the importance of background. We place events in context. Whether it's fashion, politics, or understanding why we act the way we do, you always have to look at the past."*

The scientist: *"Human beings are an incredibly vain*

species—obtuse and self-centered. They refuse to believe that the world works the way it does when that belief diminishes their own importance. People still haven't accepted evolutionary theory—I mean really accepted it in their hearts, not just intellectually. Why not? Because they won't acknowledge that their ancestors weren't always human. And they won't acknowledge that life is purely physical. Art, music, politics, relationships— everything is a matter for scientific study."

Professional blinders obscure your peripheral vision and limit your scope. Take them off. The wider your perspective, the more you'll see. (What's with these other professionals? Don't they realize that everything, finally, is a philosophical problem?)

The Courage of Your Convictions

Judging the issues objectively is difficult, as this chapter has tried to show. Difficult does not mean impossible. After all, we're entitled to our convictions, and convictions are by nature firmly held. When you believe something, you believe it's true: You wouldn't say, "I believe that the Cardinals won the pennant last year even though, in truth, they didn't." When you believe something is true, you also believe that opposing points of view are false.

This is where we get nervous. We're comfortable insisting that we're right, but we're uneasy insisting that others are wrong. My teacher Sidney Hook, the pragmatist philosopher, once remarked to our class: "Either all religions are wrong, or just one is right." In true egalitarian spirit, we wanted to believe that every religion has its own special insight. Hook could agree to that. His point was that if you believe that your favored religion is the true one, then you have to believe that all other religions are false. To be a traditional Christian, you must believe that Jesus is our savior and the Son of God. If you believe that about Jesus, you simply cannot be an observant Muslim because Islam rejects the notion that God had a son and the existence of anyone superior to Muhammad. You can't be both a practicing Jew and a practicing Hindu.

This exclusivity applies to our moral beliefs as well. To judge an act immoral is to judge its defenders morally in the wrong. Because this strikes us as arrogant we back off from our certitude, muttering, "Well, it's morally wrong for me, but perhaps it's morally right for you." This statement is as meaningless as saying, "Force equals mass X acceleration for me but not for you. You have your physics and I have my physics."

When you buy a pair of brown oxfords you aren't committing yourself to the idea that everyone should buy an identical pair of shoes. On the other hand, when you return a lost wallet because you think that's the right thing to do, you do what you believe everyone in a similar situation should do. That's what makes it a *moral* decision as opposed to just a whim or a practical preference. To adopt a moral stance is to take a position for all human beings in similar situations. This doesn't mean you should take a sledgehammer to anyone who disagrees with you. It does mean that having a conviction entails thinking that those who disagree with you are wrong. When we speak of the "courage of your convictions," the courageous part isn't asserting that you're right—that's easy. The courageous part is asserting that others are wrong.

PART IV

The Integrity of Your Values

9

Nine Misleading Moral Clichés
(and Their Cures)

Pick up any writing manual and you'll find a warning against the use of clichés. Clichés, you're cautioned, are for lazy writers. Surely you can find a more vigorous way to make your point than by resorting to a tired commonplace. Moral clichés, too, are readily available and appeal to lazy thinkers. But unlike verbal clichés—whose sin, at worst, is boring writing—moral clichés can have serious consequences.

Their danger lies in the temptation they present to solve complex problems with quick, easy slogans. The political philosopher Hannah Arendt wrote a provocative treatise on the banality of evil, and we could say as much about the evil of banality. Moral clichés make us instantly comfortable, and that should be immediate grounds for suspicion.

In a society not much given to moral reflection, moral clichés abound. No doubt with a little effort you could construct your own list of trite, deceptively profound maxims. In any case, here's my list of current favorites. Some of these clichés are vacuous, some counterproductive, and some downright harmful. Insofar as they purport to provide some deep moral truth but don't, all of them are misleading.

Why nine clichés? Because ten is such a cliché.

―――――――

1. What Goes Around Comes Around

This cliché suggests that the good you do will return to benefit you and the harm will come back to hurt you. Live a righteous life and life will do right by you; act unfairly to others, and your own life will be miserable. The evidence in support of this equation is, alas, nonexistent. Nonexistent may be putting it too strongly; they say every joke has some truth to it, and so does every cliché. Spend your life badmouthing others and others will snipe at you. Unscrupulous people don't attract nice people, and everyone is wary of a gossip. It's also true, however, that bullies often get their way, the dishonest become wealthy, and the ambitious attain the fame they crave.

When it comes to the important things in life, moral goodness seems to matter even less. Very bad things do happen to very good people, and vice versa. Think of the decent couple with the severely retarded child, or the wonderful woman in the prime of her life brought down by breast cancer, or the industrious, talented worker fired unjustly from his job. And very good things happen to very bad people. Think of the scoundrel enjoying the winter days on his yacht in the Caribbean. The memory of the suffering he has inflicted on others doesn't disturb his peace of mind one bit.

Other versions of this misleading maxim are the aphorisms "Honesty pays" and "Honesty is the best policy." These slogans not only encourage wishful thinking, but also distort the premises of morality. Take a walk down an inner-city street and see who's flashing the cash—the hardworking mother of three or the drug-pushing pimp? Perhaps you have no interest in taking that walk, but young children in that community do it every day. They learn early that it isn't honesty that pays, but crime—what doesn't pay is getting caught. We learn the same lesson when we read about the financial shenanigans of corporate moguls.

Moral decency doesn't ensure economic success, physical health, or even emotional stability. It isn't supposed to. When you think of it, it's incredible that we would want to sell morality as a good business policy. It's just the other way around—we need to be moral even when being so entails personal sacrifice. Isn't that the whole point of a commitment to morality?

The Talmud relates a wonderful anecdote that captures this essential point:

A Rabbi committed an infraction, grave enough to call down a judgment from Above. The Divine voice notified the Rabbi that because of his sin he had forfeited his place in heaven. He would be barred from Paradise in the world to come.

Upon hearing this judgment, the Rabbi burst into a joyous dance. Perplexed, his students asked him how he could be so cheerful upon hearing that he was refused entry into Paradise. The Rabbi explained: "All my life, I always suspected that my good deeds had an ulterior motive. Whenever I fulfilled the commandments, I envisioned the reward I would receive for my good

*deeds. Now, for the first time, I can serve God purely without
any personal hidden agenda."*

The good we do does not automatically result in tangible
advantages. A less sanguine cliché comes closer to capturing
the truth: "Life is not fair." This maxim reflects not cynicism
but hard-edged recognition of the sheer randomness of our
fortunes.

2. Let Your Conscience Be Your Guide

"Do what you think is right." As opposed to what—do what
you think is wrong? When you *choose* to act morally—which
many of us often don't, for various reasons—doing the right
thing always means doing what you think is morally right.
That's just tautology masquerading as wisdom. Even in circumstances where you're inclined to do one thing but decide
to follow the contrary judgment of someone else, it's still *you*
who make the decision.

The motto "Let your conscience be your guide" does hint
at more substance than just telling people to do what they
think is right. It assumes some magical source for morality:
your conscience. Unfortunately, this appeal to conscience
melts under the heat of real-life moral choices.

Let's suppose that Rita is an absolute pacifist. She believes
that it's immoral to kill even in self-defense, and that it's
certainly immoral to kill as part of a military campaign. You,
however, want to join the Army to fight in a war that you
consider eminently justified. You ask Rita what she thinks
you ought to do. She now has a problem. On the one hand,

she is morally opposed to military service, but on the other hand, she is morally committed to the (meta)principle that everyone should follow his conscience. Here your conscience tells you to join the Army. How can Rita reconcile her contradictory beliefs?

She can't. She might reply that you're misreading your conscience, because a true conscience would never tell you to act immorally and fight in wars. According to this view, we all have the same conscience "deep down," but some of us just aren't getting the message. The obvious problem with this dodge is, Who decides who has the correct reading of the true universal conscience? Who decides whose conscience is right and whose conscience is wrong?

Here's the real point. No one tells you to follow your conscience when your conscience tells you to kill all the redheads in Des Moines. People tell you to follow your conscience only when it tells you to do what *they* find morally acceptable. Don't expect those who vehemently oppose abortion, say, to advise you to follow your conscience when your conscience tells you to have an abortion. You're asking them to grant you the prerogative to commit an act they consider grossly immoral, and that they can't and won't do. The appeal to conscience doesn't help you arrive at moral truth. To act morally you must figure out what you should do and then do it because you ought to. Telling people to follow their consciences is of no use at all.

3. All's Fair in Love and War

It's just the other way around. Moral rules are never more important than in matters of love and war. Typically, people proclaim that all's fair in love and war to justify their own unethical behavior or their country's unethical behavior. You rarely hear this cliché from the victims of aggression. So the first thing to notice about this platitude is its intellectual dishonesty; the second is its noxiousness.

Wars kill. That tells you right away that morality matters here. You can't take someone's life and not consider the moral ramifications. Indeed, throughout history, a few ugly exceptions aside, opposing armies respected certain moral ground rules. Even the most bellicose states feel the need to justify their aggression by claiming self-defense. And all armies recognize, at least in principle, a moral difference between killing civilians and killing soldiers (the word "innocent" in the phrase "innocent civilians" already indicates a special moral status), as well as rules for the treatments of prisoners and prohibitions against biological and chemical weapons.

Moral guidelines in war are difficult to formulate: Do severe economic pressures justify violence? Are civilians who work in munitions production noncombatants? Is a nuclear weapon more morally acceptable than biological warfare? These aren't rhetorical questions.

Close on the heels of this cliché comes the maxim "Might makes right." Social Darwinists view all of life as a competition for survival in which the winner dictates the moral rules. According to this cynical notion, the only thing wrong with the Nazis is that they lost the war. It's true that "history is written by the victor"—extinct and powerless civilizations are in no position to set up their own value systems as the standards by which to judge others. But it's not true that victors never admit that they were the bad guys. Most contemporary Americans, for example, acknowledge that their country acted horrendously in its earlier treatment of American Indians and African-Americans. That triumphant societies can and do admit their own wrongdoing shows that even victors appeal to moral standards that go beyond mere conquest. Determining right and wrong on the basis of strength makes a mockery of all morality.

On to love. What does this part of the cliché mean anyway? That if you love someone, you can do anything to maintain your love? Lie? Cheat? Spy? Blackmail? Murder?

Murder, you say (I hope), goes too far. Then all is *not* fair in love. And now that we've allowed morality into the picture, we can begin to make the necessary distinctions. Because love, like war, involves people at their most vulnerable, moral sensitivity is especially important here. Indeed, I've devoted an entire chapter of this book to highlighting some of the moral problems associated with romance. Some things are fair in love and war, and some things aren't. It's our moral obligation to decide which is which.

4. All Religions Teach the Same Basic Moral Truths

What same moral truths? That it's wrong to kill? Some religions exhort the faithful to kill heretics. Other religions command the killing of witches, and still others demand capital punishment for adulterers. Is religious ethics uniform in prohibiting the murder of *innocent* people? Most secular laws have the same prohibition. What's true for murder is true for other moral principles—there is no such thing as a single religious ethic. Religions differ as much in their morality as they do in their beliefs about God and faith.

When you talk about religious ethics you must specify a particular religious tradition. Religious values in Iran are predominantly Islamic, in Calcutta Hindu, and in Tennessee Christian. What are religious values? The first problem with the term "religion" is semantic. What do we mean by religion? A long, winding road, this question, and one we can't follow here. Do be aware, however, that not all religions conceive of God as understood in Western religions. Traditional Buddhism is atheistic, Hinduism has thousands of gods, and Manichaean religions see the world as a constant struggle between the force of good and the force of evil, with no supreme God to decide the battle. Animists and pantheists don't view the gods or God as the creator of the universe but as synonymous with it. These theological differences spill over into ethical ones. You can't tell people to sacrifice their lives to the service of a god if they don't believe in one. Buddhists do not postulate a god, but they certainly preach an ethics based on their understanding of the human condition. It isn't the same ethics as Calvinism, of that you can be sure.

Let's turn to Western religions. The three major Western religions, in chronological order, are Judaism, Christianity, and Islam. These theistic religions not only believe that God exists and that He wants us to live our lives a certain way, but also that He's already *told* us how to live our lives. When did God reveal His will? That depends on your religious persuasion. For Jews, God revealed His will when He gave the Torah to Moses at Mount Sinai; for Christians, God's will is manifested in the life of Jesus; for Muslims, God's will is found in the Koran as dictated to Muhammad in the cave.

All three major Western religions share many values and oppose much of the teaching of Eastern religions—the fatalism and the caste system of Hinduism, for example. But you'll also find significant differences between the Western religions themselves when you get down to specifics—and that's where the action is, after all. The Catholic prohibition against divorce strikes Jews and Muslims as harsh, Islamic restrictions on women are abhorrent to non-Muslims, and many Christians and Muslims are offended by the tribal underpinnings of Jewish ethics.

"Religious ethics" paints with too broad a brush. You can find secular humanist support for most religious moral precepts, and, conversely, almost every secular moral principle is echoed somewhere in the religious ranks. When you refer to religious values, you must be specific. There is no religious moral tradition "in general."

5. Natural Is Morally Better

"Chemicals. The stuff is full of chemicals." Her lip curls. Disgusting. But everything, of course, is made of chemicals . . . the universe is chemical. That's not what she means, of course. What she means is that the products of nature are inherently better than the products of the laboratory.

This cliché is a popular plank in the ecology movement. Proponents preach that destroying nature is not only unwise but is also immoral. The notion that nature has moral content is not new. Many have maintained that contraception, incest, homosexuality, genetic engineering, surrogate motherhood, euthanasia, etc., are all immoral because they are unnatural. What's unnatural? Deviation from the norm? In that case, married couples who have sex more than three times a week—the average frequency—are engaged in unnatural and, therefore, immoral sexual behavior. People with I.Q.'s higher than 100 are statistically above average. Are they unnatural? Immoral? The idea is absurd. If unnatural means everything that isn't found in nature, then T-shirts are unnatural, ice cream is unnatural, and so is a pair of eyeglasses. Are these artifices immoral?

The more closely we examine what we mean by natural, the cloudier the concept becomes. Nature sustains life and we'd be foolish to disrupt a system that has been around for billions of years. But nature also destroys life, bringing us earthquakes, floods, and germs that cause slow, painful deaths. It would be suicidal to upset nature's fine balance, but it would also be suicidal to become nature's willing victims.

Sometimes this exhortation to preserve nature is couched in the language of rights—the rights of animals, plants, trees, and rivers. Confusion is rampant here. We should preserve the whales. But do two whales have a greater right to life than, say, four hundred squirrels? Yes, some would answer, because whales are becoming extinct and extinction is forever. But we need to remember that billions of species have inhabited the earth during the last three and a half billion years—and 99 percent of them are extinct! This is the way our beloved nature works. We care more about whales than we do about cockroaches or bacteria because we want our grandchildren to experience these wonderful animals. This desire is a sensible appeal to the interests of humans, not the interests of animals.

Another appeal to the integrity of nature is the admonition not to play God. According to this principle, we have no business fooling with people's deaths or their genes. That decision belongs to nature or God. But this blanket refusal to get involved in life-and-death issues reflects a deep moral cowardice. It's also unrealistic—we can't always avoid making these decisions. Aren't we playing God when we operate on a ruptured appendix? Are we supposed to let nature take its course and allow the person to die? Humans always act to change nature, sometimes to their benefit, sometimes to their detriment. It's natural for us to act this way. Nature is morally neutral. We are not.

6. Love Humanity

I love mankind; it's people I can't stand.

—Charles Schulz

Forget about loving *humanity*. You can't love humanity because humanity doesn't exist. Many philosophers believe this is literally true: There is no such object as humanity. There is you, there is I, there is the other guy, but there is no such entity as humanity. "Humanity," "the human race," "mankind" are just terms we use to describe the set of all *Homo sapiens*, a species each of whose members are specific people.

Let's not squabble over semantics. Whether or not mankind exists in some metaphysical sense, it's not something you can love. Love is a special relationship. It entails selecting an individual from the crowd as the object of your affection. Therefore, to love everyone is to reject the particularity of this relationship and to distort the whole point of love. (Perhaps you can love humanity as opposed to loving beavers or rocks, but that's hardly an imposing moral principle. I suppose, too, that God can love mankind. One wag remarked: "Do you know why we have a Bible? Because when told that God is Love, one smart guy said, 'Get it in writing.' " Notice, in any case, that even in the realm of the Divine, the billboard proclaims that Jesus loves you, not that Jesus loves humanity.)

Here's why all this matters: In general, the devotion to humanity is often a mask for an inability to connect to other people on a personal level. Some of the greatest "lovers of mankind" have downright ugly histories when it comes to their personal relationships. Marx, for example, wouldn't care for his child, and Rousseau and his mistress deposited their five illegitimate babies on the steps of a foundling home. These intellectuals—the list of those like them is long—had an enormous impact on the history of the world, but I doubt whether a love of people as individuals is the right way to characterize their motivation. Nor should we forget that ruthless dictators always justify their butchery as necessary to achieve their cherished goal of saving mankind. If you get nervous around people who proclaim their love for the human race, your intuitions are probably working well.

The weakness of the moral dictum to love mankind points to an important feature of morality: *Our emotions are directed to individuals, not abstractions.* We learn moral lessons from specific cases rather then from generalities. Great writers understand the esssential specificity of our lives—that we extract universal insights from the particular. Dostoyevski didn't write about human beings "in general" but about particular Russians living in a particular time and place. Advertisers also know that numbers don't sell. When charitable organizations try to get you to cough up some money for their cause, they don't say that ten thousand children are hungry; they show you a picture of one actual starving child. You can't love an abstraction, which is why loving humanity is loving no one at all.

7. There Are Two Sides to Every Moral Issue

This cliché is based on misplaced tolerance and a sense of fairness gone awry. Not every view deserves equal respect. Nancy is getting divorced. She has a horror story to tell about her husband, Paul. Not so fast, you warn yourself. There are two sides to every tale. Fairness dictates that you hear Paul's version before you condemn him. Here's where the confusion sets in. You need to hear both sides, but having done so, you no longer have to accord the same moral standing to both parties. That both claim the truth doesn't imply that both possess the truth—or even part of it.

We often forget this and rush to declare moral equivalency any time we confront a disagreement. We read about a political conflict between countries and immediately assume that a just solution is somewhere in the middle, thereby confusing justice with politics. Political reality directs us to split the difference because politics is about compromise, not justice. At the root of this cliché is a common logical muddle. We're committed to the idea that everyone has equal rights, and then, ludicrously, stretch the same equality to the arguments themselves: Since everyone has an equal right to his view, every view is equally right!

This attachment to evenhandedness is bolstered by another philosophical confusion: If we can't know the truth, there is no truth. Truth, however, doesn't depend on the state of our knowledge. No one knows Shakespeare's blood type, and, presumably, no one ever will, but you can be sure that he had one. The jury may not be able to decide whether the defendant did or didn't shoot the victim, but the reality is that he either did or didn't. Paul either is or isn't guilty of all those horrible things that Nancy accuses him of doing. Your desire to accept *both* Paul's and Nancy's version of events doesn't change that reality.

When faced with a conflict, we find ourselves righteously intoning that no side is completely right. Why not? Claiming a right doesn't give you a right. In fact, some views don't even deserve to be heard in the first place, and extending this honor to them makes a mockery of moral judgment.

―――――

8. You Are Responsible for Your Disease

"Did you hear? Joe's got cancer. It's sad, but not surprising when you consider the way he lived, working all the time, caught up in a constant whirl. You live that way, you can't hear your body's demands. You live that way, you get cancer."

Poor Joe. Not only is the fellow dying of cancer, but people are blaming him for his own disease. Blaming the sick for their sickness is not only unscientific but mean-spirited as well. That's what makes this cliché so upsetting, and you hear it repeated even among the sophisticated and caring.

Let's quickly knock down the obvious straw men. Clearly, if you smoke cigarettes you have no right to be surprised if you get lung cancer. If you have a history of coronary problems in your family, puff two packs a day, and eat a pound of pistachio nuts every night to add to your already hefty poundage, you clearly contribute to your heart problems. This irresponsibility can have a moral component: If you're forty-five and the parent of three children, you have a moral obligation not to kill yourself trying to satisfy minor cravings.

Admittedly, some people have habits that are detrimental to their health, but it's absurd to conclude from this that *all* disease is self-caused. There's not a shred of hard evidence to support the notion that Joe's intense work schedule caused his cancer. Moreover—and this is an important qualification—the fact that an ill person led an unhealthy life is no reason to condemn him with a cruel "You asked for it." No one asks to be sick.

The desire to trace illness to a moral weakness has a long history. In a number of religions, sickness has been seen as the manifestation of sin. Mary Baker Eddy founded Christian Science on this very idea: Physical infirmities are the result of spiritual infirmities. The cure for disease? No big surprise here: Clean up your spiritual life. Sin may be out of fashion, but the connection between disease and weakness of character lives on. As Susan Sontag has insightfully discussed, illness is a metaphor for evil (for example, we speak of a serious problem as "a cancer among us"). We now decry "unnatural living" and the alienation from a holistic life. These messages contain the same moralistic overtones.

Obviously, it makes sense to take care of your body, and your psychological well-being is an important component of your health. It's also obvious that even if you're conscientious and do all the right things, you may still get sick. In case you hadn't noticed, we all die: saints and sinners, carnivores and vegetarians, the fit and the flabby. The deeper reason for the popularity of attributing choice to illness is the universal desire to control nature. Those who believe in moral responsibility for disease ponderously declare, "Accidents don't happen. We make our fate." But accidents do happen. Luck is a genuine element in life. Larry walks down the street at the very moment that Vinnie throws his aquarium out the window. End of Larry.

Those committed to this cliché will blame Larry's bad karma. He's paying for his sins of another life, they'll say. At this point we leave the realm of argument and enter the realm of dogma. And dogma loses, for in the words of the illustrious graffito: "My karma ran over your dogma."

9. Moral Values Can't Be Taught

People repeat this cliché with a note of exasperation. "People are what they are, and there's nothing we can do about it." Of all moral clichés, this may be the most dangerous. Having convinced ourselves that we can't change people's values, we abdicate our responsibility to try. But we *can* change people's values, and in some cases it's our duty to make the effort.

Even those who lament that we can't teach morality must

acknowledge that, for better or worse, everyone *learns* moral values. How else do we get them? The factors that influence moral development are complex and include family, peer groups, the media, early schooling, and, according to some recent theorists, genetic makeup as well. Clearly, however, the way we teach our children values goes a long way toward determining their later moral character.

Those who defend the notion that morality can't be taught may acknowledge that we can teach ethics to children but insist that we can't teach it to adults. Once a young person has his or her values in place, that's it for life, they argue. Moral character, like personality, doesn't change. They're wrong here as well. The evidence from your own experience should dispel the notion that we're locked into any one value system. Over the years you've changed your values—changed your mind and your heart. What brought about these changes? Your emotional development, for one thing, but also your willingness to listen to new arguments, new facts, new insights. Indeed, the transformation of people's character is a basic theme of most literature.

This cliché, therefore, needs to be exploded for two reasons. First, we need to remind people that they're responsible for their moral lives and aren't prisoners of their current beliefs. We all can listen and learn. Second, we have a responsibility to teach others. In the dialogue the *Meno*, Socrates concludes that virtue is a skill and, like all skills, can be taught. How? As with so many other subjects, there is no better way to teach morality than by example.

10

The Value of Your Values

It is good to collect things, but it is better to go on walks.
                                            —Anatole France

We are owned by what we own.

                                            —Friedrich Nietzsche

Reevaluating: What Do You Want?

Some people go through their whole lives without ever asking themselves what really matters to them. Socrates had these folks in mind when he said, "The unexamined life is not worth living." Other people can't stop reassessing their goals and never get on with their lives. Of them one can say, "The unlived life isn't worth examining." For still others, anxious questions about their direction come crashing into their lives forcefully and unexpectedly. The sudden confrontation leaves them reeling: "How did I ever get to where I am now, and where am I supposed to go from here?" Most of us manage to find the time to reflect on our values, but only sporadically and in hurried bursts.

We need to ask ourselves much more systematically and honestly about what matters to us. Are you still coasting along with the same values you had when you were twenty? You've matured since then and need to make sure that your values have matured along with you. Thinking about your values is not a luxury; you live them every day of your life. Your values show up in the way you treat your friends, enemies, spouse, children, and colleagues, and they determine your politics, ethics, emotions, daydreams, life, and leisure. As you reexamine your life—and to some extent this is a lifelong process—you need to look at several crucial features of your value system.

Happiness Is Having What You Need, Not What You Want

High on everyone's list of desires is happiness. How do you discover what will make you happy? Aristotle has the right answer: *Don't look to what you want. Look to what you need.*

Anthony spends hours each day going up and down escalators. He'd be delighted, he says, to spend his life doing nothing else. Anthony may have strange cravings, you say, but hey, he's happy. Right? Wrong. To call him happy is to rob the world of all its content. The escalator freak, like the junkie with an endless supply of heroin or the miser sealed away in his attic counting his money, is not living a happy life. He is not happy even though he does what he wants. Happiness is not about satisfying just any desires. True happiness is the satisfaction of genuine needs.

What are your genuine needs? This isn't a rhetorical question. It's the key question. To begin with, not all pleasures are equal. As John Stuart Mill said, "It is better to be . . . Socrates dissatisfied than a fool satisfied." To rid yourself of painful emotions, you wouldn't opt for a frontal lobotomy that deprived you of all emotions. You wouldn't consent to being transformed into a contented grazing cow, no matter how idyllic the surroundings. Your humanity matters to you. You don't live a full human life by sitting in the corner of a room nodding out on drugs, or adding columns of numbers, or going up and down escalators. Because we're all unique individuals, we each have our own distinct needs and wishes; but because we're all people, we also share common needs that include family, friends, conversation, spirit, and passion. If the flourishing life comes with some pain, so be it.

Getting There Is Half the Fun

Determining what you need to make you happy is only half the challenge. The other half is determining how to get what you need. The Declaration of Independence guarantees everyone the right to the pursuit of happiness. Not happiness, but the *pursuit* of happiness. Jefferson understood that we can't guarantee to anyone that he will attain happiness, but we can guarantee everyone the right to try. Jefferson's dictum also contains the deeper wisdom that much of our happiness is in the pursuit itself.

When you take that walk alone on the beach and ask yourself what it would take to make you happy, your first inclination is probably to list possessions and attributes: a larger home, fame, a stronger marriage, better looks and health. How you get these commodities may seem to you to

THE PLEASURE MACHINE

Hedonism is the ethics of pleasure. According to hedonists, the ultimate good is feeling good, and the only rational and moral way to live your life is to try to have as many enjoyable experiences as possible. Hedonism sounds appealing at first—what, after all, could be wrong with pleasure? On second thought, however, many of us are offended by the utter selfishness of personal hedonism. As the following imaginary pleasure machine (a thought experiment derived from an idea of Harvard philosopher Robert Nozick) illustrates, there is an even deeper and more intriguing problem inherent in living a life devoted solely to enjoyment. Pleasure, it turns out, isn't enough.

As we know, all sensation takes place in the brain. You say your foot hurts, but the actual discomfort takes place in your brain—no brain, no pain. No brain, no pleasure, either, nor any other feelings, for that matter. Suppose we've figured out how to produce, on demand, particular sensations by directly stimulating the appropriate clusters of brain cells. This isn't a crazy notion. Neuroscientists have already made enormous strides in this very area of research.

Do you want the taste of pizza? You've got it—and without the calories! And as long as you're asking, why not the sensations of an orgasm? Why not, indeed? We excite the appropriate brain cells and the experience is yours. In front of you sits a keyboard arranged so that each note produces a distinct pleasurable sensation. Press the middle C and you'll feel as if you're having your back scratched; D-sharp at the bottom provides the delightful smell of a bouquet of roses; the G-flat two octaves up simulates the sensation of floating in water. If you have a talent for this sort of thing, you can play chords. Now you can simultaneously enjoy the pleasures of a fine wine, the sounds of a beautiful hymn, and that exquisite orgasm.

All these delightful experiences are yours if you agree to spend your entire life in the room with the pleasure machine. Do we have a deal? Perhaps you hesitate. You say that a life of mere physical pleasures isn't enough. In that case, we'll sweeten the offer. With our recent advances in virtual reality, we can provide you with an even wider range of experiences. Right here in this room, you can live out all your fantasies. You can experience the sensations of conducting a complicated piece of neurosurgery, or a Beethoven symphony, or accepting this year's Academy Award, or performing a spellbinding dance number in front of an adoring audience. How about rocking the crowd with your dazzling guitar riffs? Name your dream experience and we'll plug it in for you.

The catch, of course, is that none of this is real. All of these intense adventures are illusory. Should that make a difference? Not if you're a confirmed hedonist. A hedonist cares about feeling good, and this machine provides just what he wants. But you won't agree to the deal if you think of life as more than a collection of brain events. You'll insist on living your life in the world, not enclosed in a room. Reality matters.

be a minor detail. It's not. Chess players are a competitive breed and love to win, but no serious player would enjoy beating Kasparov, the current reigning champion, through subterfuge. No challenger would, for example, permit someone to spike Kasparov's drink. What would be the point? The chess player wants to demonstrate his skill at chess, not his skill at cheating. It always matters *how* you win. Suppose you crave fame. You fantasize about walking into a restaurant and having every head turn in your direction and every voice drop to a whisper—"That's her! She just won an Oscar for best screenplay!" But would you enjoy that fame if a ghostwriter created all of your acclaimed scripts? No, you'd feel like a fraud. You want fame, but only deserved fame, a fame that affirms *your* achievements. Similarly, you may want to be rich, but not by stealing from someone else.

Every worthwhile destination requires a journey, and a journey without a destination is just a guarantee for getting lost. Your happiness must include both your goals and the pursuit of those goals. Let's take a closer look at how we determine what matters to us.

Instrumental and Intrinsic Goods

Wisdom is the ability to make distinctions. When it comes to values, the first critical distinction is between means and ends, or what philosophers call *intrinsic goods* and *instrumental goods*. An intrinsic good is something that has value in itself; your happiness, for example, is an intrinsic good. The question "Why do you want to be happy?" doesn't make very much sense—what could possibly count as an answer? An instrumental good, on the other hand, has value because it leads to an intrinsic good. Material comforts are examples of instrumental goods. The question "Why do you need a new car?" demands a response. A possible answer might be that a new car will make you seem more successful, and that will make you happy. When the payoff is worth it, we pursue instrumental goods even if it costs us. Practicing scales is a drag, but it's the only way to learn to play the piano. Going to the dentist is no fun, but it beats the pain you'll suffer if you don't go when you need to.

Perhaps this distinction between intrinsic and instrumental goods seems obvious in theory, but it isn't obvious when we look at people's daily pursuits. We constantly confuse our priorities and turn instrumental goods into intrinsic goods. Let me offer two of my friends as everyday examples of this common inversion of means and ends.

Victor is a macrobiotic fanatic. He restlessly prowls health-food stores looking for acceptable food for his next meal, sometimes driving a half hour to get the right sprouts for his salad. Food reigns supreme in Victor's consciousness.

Here's the irony. While Victor's devotion to eating healthful vegetables and legumes is laudable—most of us have terrible diets—his priorities are topsy-turvy. *We eat well to live; we don't live to eat well.* Proper diet is very important, but not all-important. Victor has turned his concern with food into an intrinsic good, when it's only an instrumental good.

Peter is a rabid audiophile. He subscribes to four audio magazines and is up on all the latest developments in the industry. He can tell you, and would love to, which speakers offer the best woofers and tweeters and how to arrange them for maximum acoustic effect. He can tell you which receivers are best for the money and which CD players are most durable. He spent countless hours and countless dollars setting up the sound system in his own house.

The problem with Peter is that, despite his protestations to the contrary, he doesn't particularly like music. He just buys what's popular. I've never seen him sit down and concentrate on any of the hundreds of CD's he owns. He cares more about the delivery system than the message.

Peter and Victor are not unusual. We all invest too much of our effort and energy on instrumental goods and too little time enjoying the intrinsic goods they're supposed to serve. And we deprive ourselves for no good reason. Most of what we need to make us happy is right there waiting for us.

How can you determine your intrinsic goods? Try this thought experiment.

You hear a special bulletin over the radio. The President of the United States is addressing the nation. His voice is somber: "My fellow Americans. I don't want to invite panic, but I believe that you are entitled to know what I know. Astronomers have determined with certainty that two weeks from today, a major meteorite, one quarter the size of the earth, will collide with our planet and destroy all life. The great experiment of human existence will soon end. I am sorry to say that we can do nothing to avert this final calamity."

An unlikely scenario, but it helps us get to the issue at heart. How would you spend those last two weeks? Your answer reveals what matters in your life. You would, no doubt, spend your final hours with the people you love— crying with them, laughing with them. You would walk the shore, lie in the meadow, reflect on your life, on what was and what could have been. You would listen to your favorite music, visit your cherished paintings, commune with your God. None of these activities costs money. All of them are things you can do today; indeed, most intrinsic goods are readily available and free.

Real life gets in the way, of course. As a philosophy professor of mine once said, "The problem with living each day of your life as if it were the last, with living a philosophy of 'eat, drink, and be merry, for tomorrow we die,' is that today is probably not your last day. Tomorrow you will probably not die. Fritter away today and when tomorrow comes, you will be unprepared." True enough—we cannot live each day as if the world will end in two weeks, but neither should we live as if our lives will never end. Unfortunately, we're prone to put our intrinsic goods on hold, sometimes forever. So make the effort to spend more time with what matters in your life.

MONEY MONEY MONEY
Money often costs too much.
—Ralph Waldo Emerson

I make the following offer to the students in my ethics class. I'll give any of them $500 if they'll break some young woman's arm (I point to a student in the back of the room). I assure them that there will be no negative repercussions for those who agree to the deal. I'm always shocked by the number of my students who say they would accept the arrangement. For double the money, they would agree to break *both* of their classmate's arms. The guilt-ridden ones promise to share some of their earnings with the victim. Sweet kids.

I then try to buy their dignity. I offer $500 if they'll go to the next classroom, knock on the door, excuse themselves, walk over to the professor, bend down and lick her shoes, thank her, and return to class. A few agree to this deal, too, but, interestingly, fewer than the number of those who are willing to enter into the arm-breaking arrangement. (It shouldn't surprise me that so many are willing to compromise their values and dignity for money. In a recent study, 23 percent of American women surveyed said they would prostitute themselves for a week for $2 million. Among American men surveyed, 25 percent said that for $2 million they would abandon their families.)

Of all the conversions of instrumental goods into intrinsic goods, the deification of money is the most commonplace and the most damaging; we are money-obsessed. We think it can buy happiness, or at least rent it. We spend most of our waking hours trying to get as much of it as we can and much of our leisure time fantasizing about how we'd spend it. We call the love of it the root of all evil, yet we envy those who have more of it than we do.

Notice how we define worth in terms of capital. We ask of someone how much he's *worth* and answer with a dollar figure. We use wealth as a criterion of value, even though we may not think we do. Here's an example. It's common these days to complain about the huge sums of money awarded to professional ball-players. Why, we ask, should Darryl Strawberry receive an annual salary of millions of dollars? Isn't it scandalous that he makes more money with twenty swings of the bat than the average cancer researcher makes in a year? Notice the implicit assumption in this objection. Strawberry's reward is considered larger than the scientist's, since he gets more money. But if money doesn't count for all that much, then why the outrage? People do cancer research because they want to do something significant. They enjoy their work. Most scientists, although perhaps not all, would rather do their research than play baseball, for any amount of money. Would you accept $20 million if, in order to collect, you had to spend the next twenty years in a jail cell? It's hard to believe, but money isn't everyone's prime motivation.

Clarify in your own mind what you find attractive about money. Is money an instrumental good or has it become one of your intrinsic goods?

Invent Your Future, Reinvent Your Past

Integrity means wholeness. People who have integrity have values that belong with one another. They make sure to discard those values that are alien to their true selves. Their politics, their family life, their friendships, their career judgments are all of a piece and reflect the same moral core. Those without that cohesive core disintegrate.

This challenge to make your life whole applies not only to your values but also to the events of your life. You don't have control over everything that happens to you, but you do have control over your interpretation of what happens to you. Your life is dotted with experiences and you *choose* how to connect the dots.

All stories, including your life story, string together separate events. In telling your story to yourself and others, you emphasize some events as crucial links in the narrative while neglecting others as irrelevant. It is in the telling and remembering that events gain their significance—you can amplify or reduce the significance of anything that happens to you by altering your attitude toward it. You've marched down many blind alleys and put your heart into projects that now seem useless to you, but you don't have to see it that way. Your life isn't a straight line—no one's is. The twists and turns got you to where you are now, and there will be many more zigs and zags to come. A thriving life is a complex story with subplots, digressions, and surprises. View your life as an expedition rather than a series of aimless meanderings.

The Pluralism of Ideals

Philosophers have a long-standing debate about the ideal life. One school insists that every individual, every age, every culture, has its own unique value system. No single notion of the good life is appropriate for everyone—there is no one right way to live a life. A second school insists that a universal ideal must prevail. Despite the differences between people, we all share the same basic aspirations and values. This is why we can read with profit the philosophies of Plato, Buddha, and Confucius. What they had to say about the human condition still makes sense because true wisdom spans continents and millennia.

Both views are right to some degree. We share basic values, but we differ as individuals in the expression of those values. Van Gogh devoted his life to painting, Emily Dickinson to poetry, Socrates to philosophical truth, Einstein to physics, Marco Polo to exploration, and Lincoln to justice. Each had his or her own life project, but all shared a passion for their work, a passion without which they would have accomplished little. Passion is a universal value, though it is expressed individually. So, too, we share other core values, although we each articulate those values in our own personal way.

In determining the central values you share with the rest of humanity, I recommend that you consider the following:

• *Beware the seduction of mass culture.* Every culture has a value system and a method of transmitting it. In traditional societies, the values are well defined and are communicated primarily through family and community. In our own modern, pluralistic society the family and community are too fractured to impart values with any consistency. The media have now filled this vacuum, becoming the central arbiter of what our culture deems important. Through messages both overt and covert, the entertainment industry defines for most people what counts as the good life. Maintaining your own vision in the face of this onslaught is a constant battle, and protecting your children from media fallout is more difficult still. It's a battle you must fight.

• *Study moral philosophy.* This is where I make a pitch for my professional discipline. Smart, dedicated men and women have thought long and hard about how we should live our lives. It would be foolish for anyone trying to think about philosophical issues to disregard the fruits of their labor. That would be like reinventing calculus from scratch—why bother when it's already been done? You won't agree with everything you read, but at least your opponents will be substantial and provocative. Do some intellectual shopping. Check out the classics as well as the contemporary thinkers. And take your time. You're looking for wisdom, not an instant fix.

• *Make your values part of something bigger.* You're a single individual with a single life, but you're also part of a family, a group of friends, a community, a country, a planet—a part of creation. You have extensive allegiances that exceed the confines of your personal self. Without this larger context, your dreams grow stale, and it becomes increasingly difficult to justify all the aggravations of life's daily struggles. Conversely, when you see your existence as part of a larger canvas, a greater endeavor, the scope and meaning of your life expand. What is this larger picture that your efforts are part of? Perhaps it's your community, or an ideology, or service to a Deity. *You* decide.

On the Virtue of Being Confused

If you're rational, morally sensitive, intellectually and spiritually honest, you're also confused. Theologians glorify the virtues of simple faith, but faith is never simple, certainly not these days. Moralists, too, always have clear-cut answers to ethical questions, but that's because they avoid complexity. If your values are open to other points of view, then you must expect to be bewildered on occasion. It isn't easy to decide what's more important: Equal distribution of opportunity or individual merit? Preserving the sanctity of life or maintaining the sanctity of one's control over one's body? Your right to live your life according to the dictates of your own wishes or your obligations to your family and community? Your responsibility toward your country or to humanity at large? Maintaining your standards of rational proof or allowing yourself to take leaps of faith? Acting maturely and sticking to your career or following your impulse to chuck it all for new adventures? We can raise such questions far into the night. Some will be easier than others to answer, but only the simpleminded will experience no conflicts at all. The appreciation of complexity is a sign of intellectual sensitivity.

Modern life offers choices, choices exacted at the cost of confusion. We're confused about moral issues, political issues, relationships, and even how to view our own lives. For example, which of the following sounds right?

A. Life is wonderful. Sure, it has its dark patches—a lot more than I'd like. I know all about widespread suffering, anger, and frustration, but on the whole, life is a tremendous adventure. There's something about the human spirit that lets it soar above all the misery below, and the challenge makes it all worthwhile.

B. Life stinks. Look, I know there's joy along the way. I'm as capable of a good laugh as the next person. I've had my share of love's ecstasies. But I also know that most people are unhappy and that there's more sorrow in life than pleasure. I also know that it ends badly for everyone. I'm not committing suicide—I'm just calling it as it is. Life is unrelenting and tough.

Both attitudes sound persuasive at different times in your life. That we can easily sympathize with both outlooks shows just how equivocal we are about our basic attitudes. It's very difficult to get a clear perspective.

Beware of the pamphleteers lurking at the door with the cure for your perplexity. They'll promise to resolve your spiritual concerns, your political dilemmas, and your moral qualms. Don't underestimate how tempting the appeal of "the simple truth" can be, especially when your life is in disarray.

You'd be trading in your questions for answers, but just when you think all is resolved, your questions will reappear more forcefully than ever. You're better off sticking with your questions, quandaries . . . and standards. *Confusion is not the end of wisdom but the beginning of wisdom.* Take heart in a profound dictum of the philosopher Ludwig Wittgenstein: "In philosophy, the winner of the race is the one who gets there last."

Who Is Leading Your Life?

Hell is to drift; heaven is to steer.
—George Bernard Shaw

When people tell you that "you have one life to lead," they usually stress the word "one," but the emphasis should really be on the word "lead." Most people don't lead their lives—they follow. They react rather than act. They make moral decisions by rote and borrow their values from those around them. They don't govern their emotions but are governed by them. To lead your life you need to assume the qualities—and risks—of leadership. Like all leaders, you must battle the comforts of inertia and overcome the forces of habit. You have to get out in front of your life, where events are never predictable but also never dull. Here are a few pivotal qualities of leadership.

• *Leaders welcome responsibility.* "It's not my fault" is the motto of children. Alas, it is also the motto of most grown-ups. The only difference is that adults are more creative in shifting responsibility away from themselves; they cast blame on their environment, their professional duties, their genetic weaknesses—any excuse will do.

In criminal law, when you commit a felony you are responsible for all that follows from that felony. The defendant might not have known that his victim had an eggshell for a skull when he intentionally hit him, but having killed the person, he is guilty of manslaughter. Leaders accept responsibility in the same way. When they make a mistake that results in unforeseen setbacks, they assume responsibility for all that results from their misjudgment. Indeed, in some political and corporate cultures, the chief executive always accepts responsibility for the blunders of his subordinates even when he had no personal involvement in their failures. Leaders of communities—and leaders of their lives—understand that broader responsibility comes with broader maturity. When you lead your life, you appeal to excuses only rarely and reluctantly, and willingly accept responsibility for all of your attitudes, emotions, and decisions.

• *Leaders take chances.* Leaders are out in front where the risks are greatest. They expect to make errors in judgment along the way. Only those who never venture never fail. Mistakes are part of the process of leadership. With regard to leading a life, this means opening yourself up to new experiences, new perspectives, and new ideas. Don't underestimate the courage you'll need to try out new beliefs. You risk looking foolish. When should you adopt a new set of values and beliefs? You need to rely on your intuitions and standards, changing when change is needed. Leaders refuse to get stuck in their lives. It's a chancier life, but it's *your* life.

• *Leaders get things done.* Leaders accomplish. Followers plan to accomplish. You can dream forever, for *someday* is never. Leaders act, they don't just talk about acting. They have realistic goals and realistic strategies for achieving those goals. Leaders want to have something to show at the end of the day. Our society is fixated on method rather than implementation. We emphasize teaching children "how" to learn, with the assumption that someday they will get around to applying this skill. Too many never do. In our personal lives, we are constantly in the process of preparing ourselves to get things done. You can easily spend your entire life preparing. Leaders get on with it.

• *Leaders practice what they preach.* A boss says, "Go!" A leader says, "Let's go!" When it comes to leading your life, this exhortation has less to do with hypocrisy than with avoiding commitment. No one lives up to all his standards. That's only natural—ideals are something you aspire to but rarely achieve. The question here is whether you're practicing your ideals in order to come closer to realizing them.

• *Leaders work out their views in the real world of action.* This is true for military leaders, business leaders, and leaders of their own lives. Values and moral principles take practice, like everything else. If you contend that the responsibility for charity belongs not with the government but with individuals, start with your own pocketbook. If you believe that we need to strengthen community spirit, become involved in community affairs. Only by practicing your convictions can you discover how you really feel about them. To lead your life, you need to practice your beliefs.

• *Leading a life is a complicated business.* You belong to a specific time, place, and culture but share universal truths with all of humankind. You find yourself constantly balancing the demands of your own survival with those of your community; charity begins at home and too often ends there. Opposing moral arguments sometimes sound equally persuasive, and you need to learn to live with confusion and doubt. You want to improve yourself but you also need to accept yourself. Leading a life is a complicated business, but it sure beats the alternative.